Salesforce To uch Platform

opment Guide

D1028655

Salesforce Touch Platform

ISBN: 978-1-4276-9555-0

Written by Mario Korf, with contributions from Michael Alderete, Alex Berg, Sandeep Bhanot, Josh Birk, Steve Bobrowski, Jack Cai, Cory Cowgill, Anita Dennis, Tom Gersic, Akhilesh Gupta, Kevin Hawkins, Mike Jacobsen, Wolfgang Mathurin, Eugene Oksman, Pat Patterson, Adam Seligman, Richard Whitley, Quinton Wall, Clive Wong, and Rob Woollen

Table of Contents

Preface

In 1981, the IBM PC was released with a 5Mhz 16 bit processor running Microsoft DOS. In 2012, the Apple iPhone 4s was released with a dual-core, 1GHz processor. Thirty years of hardware and software gave us three orders of magnitude of performance improvement -- *in our pockets*. Now, we live in a world with 2.3B internet users and 6.1B mobile phone users.

Mobile devices have radically changed the way we work and play. Workers stay in touch, connect with customers and peers, and engage on social networks and apps. Data must be consumed, created, and shared from a wide range of connected devices.

Most companies have an assortment of applications they run their businesses on, but most of these apps don't work in the mobile world. They simply aren't available in the workers' hands when they need them. HR, ERP, intranets, and custom apps are locked away. They don't provide the app experience users expect, and they aren't wired into social graphs like consumer apps.

Yesterday's platforms were not designed for the fundamental changes needed in the mobile world.

The platforms most companies have bought and built these old apps around were not built for this new world. Big monolithic stacks and rigid integration patterns don't work in this mobile world. These apps are getting replaced by cloud apps every day.

Mobile applications require fundamentally new architectures and application designs. The techniques that evolved since the 1990s for web applications on PCs don't apply in the mobile world. Enterprise mobile applications need a new, modern platform designed for the demands of mobile application development.

Table 1: Comparison of PC/Web applications and a modern mobile application

Category	Typical PC / Web application	Mobile / modern application
Connection and Availability	• Fast, reliable LAN • Low latency • High bandwidth • Connectivity assumed	• Varying connection • High latency • Low bandwidth • Offline operation required
User Interactions	• Keyboard and mouse • Long desktop interactions	• Touch screen • Quick, focused actions
Perimeter Security	• Corporate VPN or LAN access to applications	• Cumbersome to require VPN from mobile devices • IP restrictions ineffective with public mobile networks
Device Standardization	• Typically purchased and controlled by IT	• Often Bring Your Own Device (BYOD) • Multiple platforms
Form Factor	• Large (PC) screen	• Apps must support phone, tablet, and PC
Social	• Typically siloed applications • Email-based collaboration	• Native user collaboration • Intuitively share and collaborate
Multi-device	• Client-server architectures with data stored on server (Web)	• Instant sharing between devices • Data propogation between devices
Device Interaction	• Applications rarely leverage telephony, camera etc.	• Native use of mobile device's camera, contacts, calendar, and location
Location	• Rarely used in web applications	• Commonly used to both associate data with a location and filter data and services based on location

The Salesforce Touch Platform

Enterprise IT departments now face the daunting task of connecting their enterprise data and services with a mobile workforce. Salesforce faced this problem itself as it moved its enterprise CRM and service applications to the mobile world. This transformation required fundamental changes in the underlying technology and implementation to support Salesforce's applications across multiple platforms (iPad, Android, and iPhone), multiple form factors (phone, tablet, and PC) with enterprise-grade reliability, availability, and security. The lessons learned and technology built to transform Salesforce's applications for mobile are now available for any company.

The Salesforce Touch Platform is the first enterprise platform designed to address the challenges of mobile applications.

The Salesforce Touch Platform is the next-generation platform that powers Salesforce's mobile applications and enables enterprises to build their own applications.
The Salesforce Touch Platform is designed for a mobile world with applications built using modern, agile development practices. It leverages the power of the Salesforce platform and its proven security, reliability, and scale for enterprise applications.

The Salesforce Touch Platform contains three core components:

- Force.com for Touch
- Mobile Container (Salesforce Mobile SDK 1.3)
- Identity

Force.com for Touch

Force.com for Touch is a new layer of services in the Salesforce Platform focused on developing and administering enterprise mobile applications.

- Mobile REST APIs provide access to enterprise data and services, leveraging standard web protocols. Developers can quickly expose their business data as REST APIs and leverage those common APIs across their different phone, tablet, and web user interfaces. The REST APIs provide a single place to enforce access, security, common policy, and enforcement across all device types.
- Social (Chatter) REST APIs enable developers to quickly transform their applications with social networks and collaboration features. The Chatter REST APIs provide access to the feed, as well as the social graph of user connections. Mobile applications can easily consume or post items to a user or group, or leverage the social graph to enable instant collaboration between connected users.

- Mobile Policy management enables administrators to enforce their enterprise security policy on mobile applications in a world without perimeter security. Administrators can enable security features such as 2-factor authentication, device PIN protection, and password rotation, as well as enabling or disabling user access to mobile applications.
- Geolocation provides location-based information to enhance your online business processes with geospatial data. Starting with the Winter '13 release, all objects in Salesforce include a compound geolocation field. The entire platform is location-ready, allowing spatial query functionality such as radius-based searching.

Mobile Container (Salesforce Mobile SDK 1.3)

The Mobile Container can be used to develop both native Objective-C iOS or Java Android apps, or it can be used to provide a native container for HTML5-based hybrid apps. Wizards for iOS and tooling for Android are provided to easily get started building native and hybrid apps. The mobile container is implemented by the Salesforce Mobile SDK and includes:

- Native device services allow developers to easily add camera, location, and contacts into their application using a common set of APIs across a broad range of devices, including iPhone, iPad, and Android devices.
- Secure offline storage enables developers to build applications which continue to function with limited or no network connectivity. The data stored on the device is securely encrypted and safe even if the device is lost or stolen.
- Client OAuth authentication support freeing developers from having to rebuild login pages and general authentication in their mobile applications. It quickly and easily integrates mobile applications with enterprise security management.

Identity

Identity provides a single enterprise identity and sign-on service to connect mobile devices with enterprise data and services, providing the following advantages:

- Allows for single sign-on across applications and devices so users are not forced to create multiple usernames and passwords.
- A trusted identity provider that you can leverage for any enterprise platform or application.
- A Cloud Directory that enables enterprises to white label identity services and use company-speicific appearance and branding.
- The ability to utilize consumer identity providers, such as Facebook, for customer-facing applications to quickly engage with customer social data.

The Dreamforce App

The Dreamforce conference requires an application that works for thousands of users around the world, across PC browsers, tablets, and mobile devices. The app had to scale to the peak loads of a weeklong conference with tens of thousands of attendees accessing the application in real-time from their mobile devices. In other words, the app had to be *mobile-first*. Salesforce.com built the Dreamforce 2012 App on the Salesforce Touch Platform leveraging the technology you'll learn in this book.

If you used the Dreamforce 2012 App in the weeks prior to Dreamforce, you might have accessed the app with your browser or a tablet. Or if you're currently attending Dreamforce, you might be accessing the app with your mobile device. Whatever the case you get the same information in an app that was created for multiple display forms using *responsive design*.

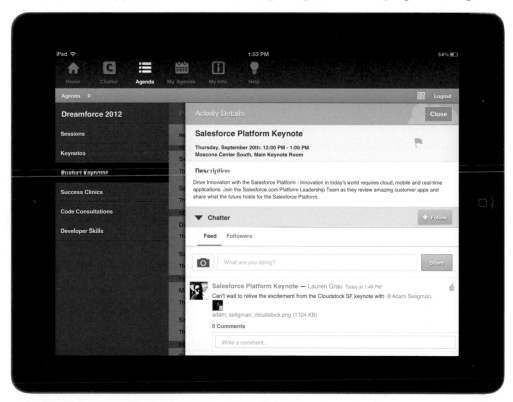

Responsive design provides an optimal user experience no matter what the device. Be it a PC browser, tablet, or mobile device, you can view and *use* the app with a minimum of resizing, panning, and scrolling, while taking advantage of the features and functionality native to the device. If you've used the Dreamforce app from more than one device, you probably already know this.

About This Book

This book introduces you to the Salesforce Touch Platform and teaches you how to architect, develop, and manage mobile applications for the cloud.

 Note: An online version of this book is available at Developer Force at `http://wiki.developerforce.com/page/Force.com_Books`.

Chapter Contents

The organization of this guide is loosely based on how you'd develop an application. This guide takes a look at architectural decisions first, then go into some important details on security, and then proceeds directly into development.

You might have noticed that native development comes first. This doesn't reflect a preference for development options; every development scenario has its time and place. But because the hybrid tutorials require some of the native setup, the chapters are ordered in reverse complexity. In other words, once you're set up for native, the rest is easy.

Thereafter the chapters take on the more complex tasks, such as caching data offline, accessing the camera, implementing social collaboration, and other fascinating etceteras. Finally it's all wrapped up with an invitation to join or Partner Program so you can list your mobile app on our AppExchange.

Version

This book was last revised on September 7th, 2012 and was verified to work with the Salesforce Winter '13 release and the Mobile SDK version 1.3.

Sending Feedback

Questions or comments about anything you see in this book? Suggestions for topics that you'd like to see covered in future versions? Go to the Force.com discussion boards at `http://boards.developerforce.com` and let us know what you think! Or email us directly at developerforce@salesforce.com.

Keeping Up to Date

To keep up to date, you should know the following.

- Whenever a new version of Salesforce is released, the Mobile section of the release notes captures all of the important details.
- This guide is updated frequently, and you can find the latest version online at `http://wiki.developerforce.com/page/Force.com_Books`. If you're reading a printed version of this guide, see Version on page 6.
- You can always find the most current Mobile SDK release in the Mobile SDK GitHub Repository.
- The latest articles, blog posts, tutorials, and webinars are on `http://wiki.developerforce.com/page/Mobile`.
- Please join the conversation on the message boards at `http://boards.developerforce.com/t5/Mobile/bd-p/mobile`.

Mobile SDK GitHub Repository

The Mobile SDK development team uses GitHub to host and store source code for the Mobile SDK. `https://github.com/forcedotcom`

You can always find the latest Mobile SDK releases in our public repositories:

- `https://github.com/forcedotcom/SalesforceMobileSDK-iOS`
- `https://github.com/forcedotcom/SalesforceMobileSDK-Android`

 Note: You might want to bookmark the Mobile SDK home page `http://wiki.developerforce.com/page/Mobile_SDK`, for the latest articles, blog posts, tutorials, and webinars.

Chapter 1

Introduction to Mobile Development on the Salesforce Touch Platform

In this chapter ...

- About Native, HTML5, and Hybrid Development
- Multi-Device Strategy
- Development Prerequisites
- Supported Browsers
- Enough Talk, I'm Ready

The Force.com platform has proven itself as an easy, straightforward, and highly productive platform for cloud computing. Developers can define application components, such as custom objects and fields, workflow rules, Visualforce pages, and Apex classes and triggers, using point-and-click tools of the Web interface, and assembling the components into killer apps. As a mobile developer, you might be wondering how you can leverage the power of the Force.com platform to create sophisticated apps.

The Salesforce Touch Platform provides essential libraries for quickly building native or hybrid mobile apps that seamlessly integrate with the Force.com cloud architecture, and simplifies development by providing:

- Device access
- Enterprise container for hybrid applications
- Geo-location
- HTML5 development
- Native REST API wrappers
- OAuth access token management
- Secure offline storage
- Social and Mobile APIs

About Native, HTML5, and Hybrid Development

Many factors play a part in your mobile strategy, such as your team's development skills, required device functionality, the importance of security, offline capability, interoperability, and so on. In the end, it's not just a question of what your app will do, but the process of how you'll get it there. The Salesforce Touch Platform offers three ways to create mobile apps:

- **Native** apps are specific to a given mobile platform (iOS or Android) and use the development tools and language that the platform supports (e.g., Xcode and Objective-C with iOS, Eclipse and Java with Android). Native apps look and perform the best.

- **HTML5** apps aren't installed from an app store, they delivered through a Web server and run in a mobile Web browser. These apps use standard Web technologies, like HTML5, JavaScript and CSS to deliver apps to any device. This write-once-run-anywhere approach to mobile development creates cross-platform mobile applications that work on multiple devices. While developers can create sophisticated apps with HTML5 and JavaScript alone, some vital limitations remain, specifically session management, secure offline storage, and access to native device functionality.

- **Hybrid** apps combine the ease of HTML5 development with the power of the native platform by wrapping a Web app inside the Salesforce Mobile Container. This approach produces an application that can leverage the device's native capabilities and be delivered through the app store. You can also create hybrid apps using Visualforce pages. Both kinds of hybrid development are covered in this guide.

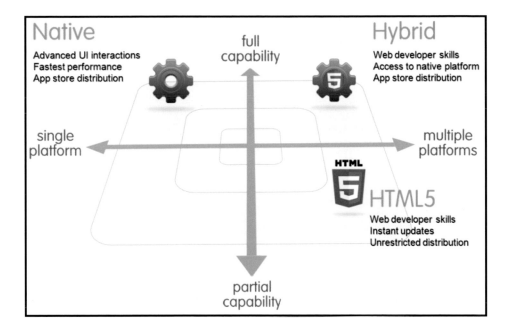

Native Apps

Native apps provide the best usability, features, and overall mobile experience. There are some things you only get with native apps:

- **Multi touch** — double taps, pinch-spread, and other compound UI gestures
- **Fast graphics API** — the native platform gives you the fastest graphics, which might not be a problem if you're showing a static screen with only a few elements, but might be an issue if you're using a lot of data and require a fast refresh.
- **Fluid animation** — related to the fast graphics API is the ability to have fluid animation. This is especially important in gaming, highly interactive reporting, or intensely computational algorithms for transforming photos and sounds.
- **Built-in components** — The camera, address book, geolocation, and other features native to the device can be seamlessly integrated into mobile apps. Another important built-in component is encrypted storage, but more about that later.
- **Ease of use** — The native platform is what people are accustomed to, and so when you add that familiarity with all of the native features they expect, you have an app that's just plain easier to use.

Native apps are usually developed using an integrated development environment (IDE). IDEs provide tools for building debugging, project management, version control, and other tools professional developers need. You need these tools because native apps are more difficult to develop. Likewise, the level of experience required is higher than other development scenarios. If you're a professional developer, you don't have to be sold on proven APIs and frameworks, painless special effects through established components, or the benefits of having your code all in one place.

HTML5 Apps

An HTML5 mobile app is basically a web page, or series of Web pages, that are designed to work on a tiny screen. As such, HTML5 apps are device agnostic and can be opened with any modern mobile browser. And because your content is on the web, it's searchable, which can be a huge benefit depending on the app (shopping, for example).

If you're new to mobile development, the technological bar is lower for Web apps; it's easier to get started here than in native or hybrid development. Unfortunately, every mobile device seems to have their own idea of what constitutes usable screen size and resolution, and so there's an additional burden of testing on different devices. Browser incompatibility is especially rife on Android devices, so browser beware.

An important part of the "write-once-run-anywhere" HTML5 methodology is that distribution and support is much easier than for native apps. Need to make a bug fix or add features? Done and deployed for all users. For a native app, there are longer development and testing cycles, after which the consumer typically must log into a store and download a new version to get the latest fix.

If HTML5 apps are easier to develop, easier to support, and can reach the widest range of devices, where do these apps lose out?

- **Offline storage** — You can implement a semblance of offline capability by caching files on the device. Even if the underlying database is encrypted, this is not as secure or as well segmented as a native keychain encryption that protects each app with a developer certificate.
- **Security** — In general, implementing even trivial security measures on a native platform can be complex tasks for a mobile Web developer. It can also be painful for users. For example, if a web app with authentication is launched from the desktop, it will require users to enter their credentials every time the app is sent to the background.
- **Native features** — the camera, address book, and other native features can't be accessed.
- **Native look and feel** — HTML5 can only emulate the native look, while users won't be able to use compound gestures they are familiar with.

Hybrid Apps

Hybrid apps are built using HTML5 and JavaScript wrapped inside a thin container that provides access to native platform features. For the most part, hybrid apps provide the best of both worlds, being almost as easy to develop as HTML5 apps with all the functionality of native.

You know that native apps are installed on the device, while HTML5 apps reside on a Web server, so you might be wondering if hybrid apps store their files on the device or on a server? Yes. In fact there are two ways to implement a hybrid app.

- **Local** - You can package HTML and JavaScript code inside the mobile application binary, in a manner similar to the structure of a native application. In this scenario you use REST APIs and Ajax to move data back and forth between the device and the cloud.
- **Server** - Alternatively, you can implement the full web application from the server (with optional caching for better performance). Your container app retrieves the full application from the server and displays it in a browser window. Visualforce hybrid applications operate in this manner.

Both types of development are covered in this guide, but in different chapters.

Native, HTML5, and Hybrid Summary

The following table sums up how the three mobile development scenarios stack up.

	Native	HTML5	Hybrid
Graphics	Native APIs	HTML, Canvas, SVG	HTML, Canvas, SVG
Performance	Faster	Slower	Slower
Look and feel	Native	Emulated	Emulated
Distribution	App store	Web	App store
Camera	Yes	No	Yes
Notifications	Yes	No	Yes
Contacts, calendar	Yes	No	Yes
Offline storage	Secure file system	Shared SQL	Secure file system, shared SQL
Geolocation	Yes	Yes	Yes
Swipe	Yes	Yes	Yes
Pinch, spread	Yes	Yes	Yes
Connectivity	Online, offline	Mostly online	Online, offline
Development skills	Objective-C, Java	HTML5, CSS, JavaScript	HTML5, CSS, JavaScript

Multi-Device Strategy

With the proliferation of mobile devices in this post-PC era, applications now have to support a variety of platforms, form factors, and device capabilities. Some of the key considerations and design options for Force.com developers looking to develop such device-independent applications are:

- Which devices and form factors should your app support?
- How does your app detect various types of devices?
- How should you design a Force.com application to best support multiple device types?

Which Devices and Form Factors Should Your App Support?

The answer to this question is dependent on your specific use case and end-user requirements. It is, however, important to spend some time thinking about exactly which devices, platforms, and form factors you do need to support. Where you end up in the spectrum of 'Support all platforms/devices/form factors' to 'Support only desktop and iPhone' (as an example) will play a major role in how you answer the subsequent two questions.

As can be expected, important trade-offs have to be made when making this decision. Supporting multiple form factors obviously increases the reach for your application. But, it comes at the cost of additional complexity both in terms of initially developing the application, and maintaining it over the long-term.

Developing true cross-device applications is not simply a question of making your web page look (and perform) optimally across different form factors and devices (desktop vs phone vs tablet). You really need to rethink and customize the user experience for each specific device/form factor. The phone or tablet version of your application very often does not need all the bells and whistles supported by your existing desktop-optimized Web page (e.g., uploading files or supporting a use case that requires many distinct clicks).

Conversely, the phone/tablet version of your application can support features like geolocation and taking pictures that are not possible in a desktop environment. There are even significant differences between the phone and tablet versions of the better designed applications like LinkedIn and Flipboard (e.g,. horizontal navigation in a tablet version vs single hand vertical scrolling for a phone version). touch.salesforce.com is another example of a user experience that is customized for a specific form factor. Think of all these consideration and the associated time and cost it will take you to support them when deciding which devices and form factors to support for your application.

Once you've decided which devices to support, you then have to detect which device a particular user is accessing your Web application from.

Client-Side Detection

The client-side detection approach uses JavaScript (or CSS media queries) running on the client browser to determine the device type. Specifically, you can detect the device type in two different ways.

- **Client-Side Device Detection with the User-Agent Header** — This approach uses JavaScript to parse out the User-Agent HTTP header and determine the device type based on this information. You could of course write your own JavaScript to do this. A better option is to reuse an existing JavaScript. A cursory search of the Internet will result in many reusable JavaScript snippets that can detect the device type based on the User-Agent header. The same cursory search, however, will also expose you to some of the perils of using this approach. The list of all possible User-Agents is huge and ever growing and this is generally considered to be a relatively unreliable method of device detection.

- **Client-Side Device Detection with Screen Size and/or Device Features** — A better alternative to sniffing User-Agent strings in JavaScript is to determine the device type based on the device screen size and or features (e.g., touch enabled). One example of this approach can be found in the open-source Contact Viewer HTML5 mobile app that is built entirely in Visualforce. Specifically, the MobileAppTemplate.page includes a simple JavaScript snippet at the top of the page to distinguish between phone and tablet clients based on the screen size of the device. Another option is to use a library like Device.js or Modernizr to detect the device type. These libraries use some combination of CSS media queries and feature detection (e.g., touch enabled) and are therefore a more reliable option for detecting device type. A simple example that uses the Modernizr library to accomplish this can be found at

  `http://www.html5rocks.com/static/demos/cross-device/feature/index.html`.
  A more complete example that uses the `Device.js` library and integrates with Visualforce can be found in this GitHub repo:

  `https://github.com/sbhanot-sfdc/Visualforce-Device.js`. Here is a snippet from the DesktopVersion.page in that repo.

```
<apex:page docType="html-5.0" sidebar="false" showHeader="false"
standardStylesheets="false" cache="false" >

<head>
  <!-- Every version of your webapp should include a list of all
  versions. -->
  <link rel="alternate" href="/apex/DesktopVersion" id="desktop"
media="only screen and (touch-enabled: 0)"/>
  <link rel="alternate" href="/apex/PhoneVersion" id="phone" media="only
 screen and (max-device-width: 640px)"/>
  <link rel="alternate" href="/apex/TabletVersion" id="tablet"
media="only screen and (min-device-width: 641px)"/>

  <meta name="viewport" content="width=device-width, user-scalable=no"/>

  <script src="{!URLFOR($Resource.Device_js)}"/>
</head>
```

```
<body>
  <ul>
    <li><a href="?device=phone">Phone Version</a></li>
    <li><a href="?device=tablet">Tablet Version</a></li>
  </ul>
  <h1> This is the Desktop Version</h1>
</body>
</apex:page>
```

The snippet above shows how you can simply include a <link> tag for each device type that your application supports and the Device.js library will take care of automatically redirecting users to the appropriate Visualforce page based on device type detected. There is also a way to override the default Device.js redirect by using the '?device=xxx' format shown above.

Server-Side Device Detection

Another option is to detect the device type on the server (i.e., in your Apex controller/extension class). Server-side device detection is based on parsing the User-Agent HTTP header and here is a small code snippet of how you can detect if a Visualforce page is being viewed from an iPhone client.

```
<apex:page docType="html-5.0" sidebar="false" showHeader="false"
cache="false"
            standardStylesheets="false"
controller="ServerSideDeviceDetection"
            action="{!detectDevice}">
  <h1> This is the Desktop Version</h1>
</apex:page>
```

```
public with sharing class ServerSideDeviceDetection {
    public boolean isIPhone {get;set;}

    public ServerSideDeviceDetection() {
        String userAgent =
System.currentPageReference().getHeaders().get('User-Agent');
        isIPhone = userAgent.contains('iPhone');
    }

    public PageReference detectDevice(){
        if (isIPhone)
            return Page.PhoneVersion.setRedirect(true);
        else
            return null;
    }
}
```

Note that User-Agent parsing in the code snippet above is far from comprehensive and you should implement something more robust that detects all the devices that you need to support based on regular expression matching. A good place to start is to look at the RegEx included in the detectmobilebrowsers.com code snippets.

How Should You Design a Force.com Application to Best Support Multiple Device Types?

Finally, once you know which devices you need to support and how to distinguish between them, what is the optimal application design for delivering a customized user experiences for each device/form factor? Again, a couple of options to consider.

For simple applications where all you need is for the same Visualforce page to display well across different form factors, a responsive design approach is an attractive option. In a nutshell, Responsive design uses CCS3 media queries to dynamically reformat a page to fit the form factor of the client browser. You could even use a responsive design framework like Twitter Bootstrap to achieve this.

Another option is to design multiple Visualforce pages, each optimized for a specific form factor and then redirect users to the appropriate page using one of the strategies described in the previous section. Note that having separate Visualforce pages does not, and should not, imply code/functionality duplication. A well architected solution can maximize code reuse both on the client-side (by using Visualforce strategies like Components, Templates etc.) as well as the server-side (e.g., encapsulating common business logic in an Apex class that gets called by multiple page controllers). An excellent example of such a design can be found in the same open-source Contact Viewer application referenced before. Though the application has separate pages for its phone and tablet version (`ContactsAppMobile.page` and `ContactsApp.page` respectively), they both share a common template (`MobileAppTemplate.page`), thus maximizing code and artifact reuse. The figure below is a conceptual representation of the design for the Contact Viewer application.

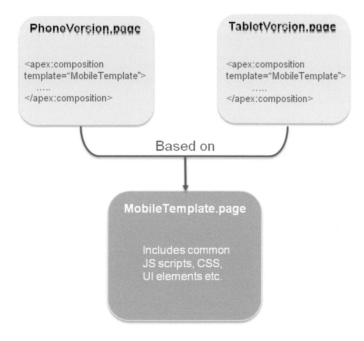

Lastly, it is also possible to service multiple form factors from a single Visualforce page by doing server-side device detection and making use of the 'rendered' attribute available in most Visualforce components (or more directly, the CSS 'display:none/block' property on a <div> tag) to selectively show/hide page elements. This approach however can result in bloated and hard-to-maintain code and should be used sparingly.

Development Prerequisites

It's helpful to have some experience with Database.com or Force.com. You'll need either a Database.com account or a Force.com Developer Edition organization.

This guide also assumes you are familiar with the following platforms and technologies:

- To build iOS applications, you'll need Mac OS X Snow Leopard or Lion, and Xcode 4.2+.
- To build Android applications, you'll need the Java JDK 6, Eclipse, Android ADT plugin, and the Android SDK.
- To build hybrid applications, you'll need an organization that has Visualforce.
- Most of our resources are on GitHub, a social coding community. You can access all of our files in our public repository, but we think it's a good idea to join. https://github.com/forcedotcom

Choosing Between Database.com and Force.com

You can build mobile applications that store data on a Database.com or Force.com organization. Hereafter, this guide assumes you are using a Force.com Developer Edition that uses Force.com login end points such as `login.salesforce.com`. However, you can simply substitute your Database.com credentials in the appropriate places.

 Note: If you choose to use Database.com, you can't develop any Visualforce–driven apps.

Sign Up for Force.com

1. In your browser go to `http://developer.force.com/join`.
2. Fill in the fields about you and your company.
3. In the `Email Address` field, make sure to use a public address you can easily check from a Web browser.

4. Enter a unique `Username`. Note that this field is also in the *form* of an email address, but it does not have to be the same as your email address, and in fact, it's usually better if they aren't the same. Your username is your login and your identity on `developer.force.com`, and so you're often better served by choosing a username that describes the work you're doing, such as `develop@workbook.org`, or that describes you, such as `firstname@lastname.com`.

5. Read and then select the checkbox for the `Master Subscription Agreement`.

6. Enter the Captcha words shown and click **Submit Registration**.

7. In a moment you'll receive an email with a login link. Click the link and change your password.

Sign Up for Database.com

1. In your browser go to `www.database.com`.

2. Click **Signup**.

3. Fill in the fields about you and your company.

4. In the `Email Address` field, make sure to use a public address you can easily check from a Web browser.

5. The `Username` field is also in the *form* of an email address, but it does not have to be the same as your actual email address, or even an email that you use. It's helpful to change the username to something that describes the use of the organization. In this workbook we'll use admin-user@workbook.db.

6. Enter the Captcha words shown

7. Read and then select the checkbox for the `Master Subscription Agreement` and supplemental terms.

8. Click **Sign Up**.

9. After signing up, you'll be sent an email with a link that you must click to verify your account. Click the link.

10. Now supply a password, and a security question and answer.

Supported Browsers

Salesforce supports the following browsers:

Browser	Comments
Microsoft® Internet Explorer® versions 7, 8, 9, and 10	If you use Internet Explorer, we recommend using the latest version. Apply all Microsoft hotfixes. Note these restrictions: • The compatibility view feature in Internet Explorer is not supported. • The Metro version of Internet Explorer 10 is not supported. For configuration recommendations, see "Configuring Internet Explorer" in the online help.
Mozilla® Firefox®, most recent stable version	Salesforce.com makes every effort to test and support the most recent version of Firefox. For configuration recommendations, see "Configuring Firefox" in the online help.
Google Chrome™, most recent stable version	Google Chrome applies updates automatically; salesforce.com makes every effort to test and support the most recent version. There are no configuration recommendations for Chrome. Chrome is not supported for the Console tab or the **Add Google Doc to Salesforce** browser button.
Google Chrome Frame™ plug-in for Microsoft® Internet Explorer® 6 and 7	Supported plug-in for Internet Explorer 6 and 7 only. Google Chrome Frame applies updates automatically; Salesforce supports only the most recent version. For configuration recommendations, see "Installing Google Chrome Frame for Microsoft® Internet Explorer®" in the online help. Chrome Frame plug-in is not supported for the Service Cloud console or Forecasts.
Apple® Safari® version 5.1.x on Mac OS X	There are no configuration recommendations for Safari. Apple Safari on iOS is not supported. Safari is not supported for the Salesforce CRM Call Center CTI Toolkit or the Service Cloud console.

Note: Salesforce uses the following domains to deliver content. If your users are allowed general access to the Internet, there is no required action. If you whitelist domains, you must add these to your list of allowed domains. If you've disabled third-party cookies (typically enabled by default in all major browsers), you must accept them for Salesforce to function properly.

- *.staticforce.com
- *.content.force.com
- *.force.com
- *.salesforce.com

 Important: For all browsers you must enable JavaScript, cookies, and SSL 3.0.

Some third-party Web browser plug-ins and extensions can interfere with the functionality of Chatter. If you experience malfunctions or inconsistent behavior with Chatter, disable all of the Web browser's plug-ins and extensions and try again.

Salesforce.com recommends a minimum screen resolution of 1024 x 768 for the best possible user experience. Screen resolutions smaller than 1024 x 768 may cause issues displaying Salesforce features such as Report Builder and Page Layout Editor.

Refer to the documentation for those products for specific information. Other requirements can be found in Salesforce System Requirements.

Enough Talk, I'm Ready

If you'd rather read about the details later, there are Quick Start topics in this guide for each native development scenario. There's also a Mobile SDK Workbook that walks you through downloading and running a simple mobile app in each platform, and for each development scenario.

- iOS Native Quick Start on page 48
- Android Native Quick Start on page 52
- Hybrid Apps Quick Start on page 59
- Download the Mobile SDK Workbook from https://github.com/forcedotcom/SalesforceMobileSDK-Samples

Chapter 2

Authentication, Security, and Identity in Mobile Apps

In this chapter ...

- OAuth2 Authentication Flow
- Creating a Remote Access Application

Secure authentication is essential for enterprise applications running on mobile devices. OAuth2 is the industry-standard protocol that allows secure authentication for access to a user's data, without handing out the username and password. It is often described as the valet key of software access: a valet key only allows access to certain features of your car: you cannot open the trunk or glove compartment using a valet key.

The Salesforce OAuth2 implementation can quickly and easily be embedded by mobile app developers. The implementation uses an HTML view to collect the username and password, which are then sent to the server. A session token is returned and securely stored on the device for future interactions.

OAuth2 Authentication Flow

The authentication flow depends on the state of authentication on the device.

First Time Authentication Flow

1. User opens a mobile application.
2. An authentication dialog/window/overlay appears.
3. User enters username and password.
4. App receives session ID.
5. User grants access to the app.
6. App starts.

Ongoing Authentication

1. User opens a mobile application.
2. If the session ID is active, the app starts immediately. If the session ID is stale, the app uses the refresh token from its initial authorization to get an updated session ID.
3. App starts.

PIN Code Authentication

1. User opens a mobile application after not using it for some time.
2. If the elapsed time exceeds the configured PIN timeout value, a PIN entry screen appears. User enters the PIN.

    Note: PIN is a function of the mobile policy - it can be shown whether you are online or offline, if enough time has elapsed since you last used the application.

3. App re-uses existing session ID.
4. App starts.

OAuth 2.0 User-Agent Flow

The user-agent authentication flow is used by client applications residing on the user's mobile device. The authentication is based on the user-agent's same-origin policy.

In the user-agent flow, the client application receives the access token in the form of an HTTP redirection. The client application requests the authorization server to redirect the user-agent to another web server or local resource accessible to the user-agent, which is capable of extracting the access token from the response and passing it to the client application. Note that the token response is provided as a hash (#) fragment on the URL. This is for security, and prevents the token from being passed to the server, as well as to other servers in referral headers.

This user-agent authentication flow doesn't utilize the client secret since the client executables reside on the end-user's computer or device, which makes the client secret accessible and exploitable.

 Warning: Because the access token is encoded into the redirection URI, it might be exposed to the end-user and other applications residing on the computer or device.

If you are authenticating using JavaScript, call `window.location.replace();` to remove the callback from the browser's history.

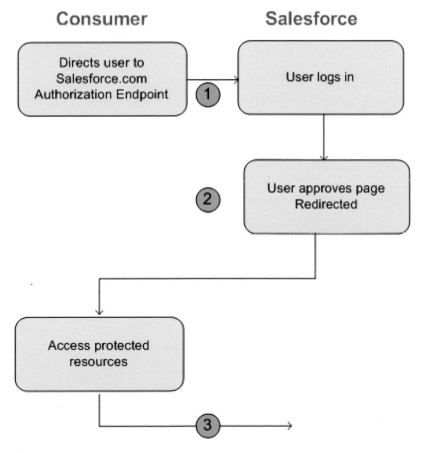

1. The client application directs the user to Salesforce to authenticate and authorize the application.

25

> **2.** The user must always approve access for this authentication flow. After approving access, the application receives the callback from Salesforce.

After a consumer has an access token, they can use the access token to access data on the end-user's behalf and receive a refresh token to get a new access token if it becomes invalid for any reason.

OAuth 2.0 Refresh Token Flow

After the consumer has been authorized for access, they can use a refresh token to get a new access token (session ID.) This is only done after the consumer already has received a refresh token using either the Web server or user-agent flow. It is up to the consumer to determine when an access token is no longer valid, and when to apply for a new one. Bearer flows can only be used after the consumer has received a refresh token.

The following are the steps for the refresh token authentication flow. More detail about each step follows:

1. The consumer uses the existing refresh token to request a new access token.

2. After the request is verified, Salesforce sends a response to the client.

Scope Parameter Values

The `scope` parameter enables you to fine-tune what the client application can access in a Salesforce organization. The valid values for `scope` are:

Value	Description
api	Allows access to the current, logged-in user's account over the APIs, such as REST API or Bulk API. This also includes `chatter_api`, allowing access to Chatter API resources.
chatter_api	Allows access to only the Chatter API resources.
full	Allows access to all data accessible by the logged-in user. `full` does not return a refresh token. You must explicitly request the `refresh_token` scope to get a refresh token.
id	Allows access only to the identity URL service. See "Using Identity URLs" in the online help.
refresh_token	Allows a refresh token to be returned if you are eligible to receive one.

Value	Description
`visualforce`	Allows access to Visualforce pages.
`web`	Allows the ability to use the `access_token` on the Web. This also includes `visualforce`, allowing access to Visualforce pages.

Using Identity URLs

In addition to the access token, an identity URL is also returned as part of a token response, in the `id` parameter.

The identity URL is both a string that uniquely identifies a user, as well as a RESTful API that can be used to query (with a valid access token) for additional information about the user. Salesforce returns basic personalization information about the user, as well as important endpoints that the client can talk to, such as photos for the user, and API endpoints it can access.

The format of the URL is: `https://login.salesforce.com/id/orgID/userID`, where `orgId` is the ID of the Salesforce organization that the user belongs to, and `userID` is the Salesforce user ID.

Note: For Sandbox, `login.salesforce.com` is replaced with `test.salesforce.com`.

The URL must always be HTTPS.

Identity URL Parameters

The following parameters can be used with the access token and identity URL. They are used in an authorization request header or in a request with the `oauth_token` parameter. For more details, see "Using the Access Token" in the online help.

Parameter	Description
Access token	See "Using the Access Token" in the online help.
Format	This parameter is optional. Specify the format of the returned output. Valid values are: • `urlencoded` • `json` • `xml`

Parameter	Description
	Instead of using the `format` parameter, the client can also specify the returned format in an accept-request header using one of the following: • `Accept: application/json` • `Accept: application/xml` • `Accept: application/x-www-form-urlencoded` Note the following: • Wildcard accept headers are allowed. `*/*` is accepted and returns JSON. • A list of values is also accepted and is checked left-to-right. For example: `application/xml,application/json,application/html,*/*` returns XML. • The `format` parameter takes precedence over the accept request header.
Version	This parameter is optional. Specify a SOAP API version number, or the literal string, `latest`. If this value isn't specified, the returned API URLs contains the literal value `{version}`, in place of the version number, for the client to do string replacement. If the value is specified as `latest`, the most recent API version is used.
PrettyPrint	This parameter is optional, and is only accepted in a header, not as a URL parameter. Specify the output to be better formatted. For example, use the following in a header: `X-PrettyPrint:1`. If this value isn't specified, the returned XML or JSON is optimized for size rather than readability.
Callback	This parameter is optional. Specify a valid JavaScript function name. This parameter is only used when the format is specified as JSON. The output is wrapped in this function name (JSONP.) For example, if a request to `https://server/id/orgid/userid/` returns `{"foo":"bar"}`, a request to `https://server/id/orgid/userid/?callback=baz` returns `baz({"foo":"bar"});`.

Identity URL Response

After making a valid request, a **302 redirect** to an instance URL is returned. That subsequent request returns the following information in JSON format:

- `id`—The identity URL (the same URL that was queried)
- `asserted_user`—A boolean value, indicating whether the specified access token used was issued for this identity
- `user_id`—The Salesforce user ID
- `username`—The Salesforce username

- `organization_id`—The Salesforce organization ID
- `nick_name`—The community nickname of the queried user
- `display_name`—The display name (full name) of the queried user
- `email`—The email address of the queried user
- `status`—The user's current Chatter status.

    ◊ `created_date:xsd datetime` value of the creation date of the last post by the user, for example, 2010-05-08T05:17:51.000Z
    ◊ `body`: the body of the post

- `photos`—A map of URLs to the user's profile pictures

 Note: Accessing these URLs requires passing an access token. See "Using the Access Token" in the online help.

    ◊ `picture`
    ◊ `thumbnail`

- `urls`—A map containing various API endpoints that can be used with the specified user.

 Note: Accessing the REST endpoints requires passing an access token. See "Using the Access Token" in the online help.

    ◊ `enterprise` (SOAP)
    ◊ `metadata` (SOAP)
    ◊ `partner` (SOAP)
    ◊ `profile`
    ◊ `feeds` (Chatter)
    ◊ `feed_items` (Chatter)
    ◊ `groups` (Chatter)
    ◊ `users` (Chatter)
    ◊ `custom_domain`—This value is omitted if the organization doesn't have a custom domain configured and propagated (see "My Domain Overview" in the online help)

- `active`—A boolean specifying whether the queried user is active
- `user_type`—The type of the queried user
- `language`—The queried user's language
- `locale`—The queried user's locale
- `utcOffset`—The offset from UTC of the timezone of the queried user, in milliseconds
- `last_modified_date`—`xsd datetime` format of last modification of the user, for example, 2010-06-28T20:54:09.000Z

The following is a response in XML format:

```xml
<?xml version="1.0" encoding="UTF-8"?>
<user xmlns:xsi="http://www.w3.org/2001/XMLSchema-instance">
<id>http://na1.salesforce.com/id/00Dx0000001T0zk/005x0000001S2b9</id>
<asserted_user>true</asserted_user>
<user_id>005x0000001S2b9</user_id>
<organization_id>00Dx0000001T0zk</organization_id>
<nick_name>admin1.2777578168398293E12foofoofoofoo</nick_name>
<display_name>Alan Van</display_name>
<email>admin@2060747062579699.com</email>
<status>
    <created_date xsi:nil="true"/>
    <body xsi:nil="true"/>
</status>
<photos>
    <picture>http://na1.salesforce.com/profilephoto/005/F</picture>
    <thumbnail>http://na1.salesforce.com/profilephoto/005/T</thumbnail>
</photos>
<urls>

<enterprise>http://na1.salesforce.com/services/Soap/c/{version}/00Dx0000001T0zk

    </enterprise>

<metadata>http://na1.salesforce.com/services/Soap/m/{version}/00Dx0000001T0zk

    </metadata>

<partner>http://na1.salesforce.com/services/Soap/u/{version}/00Dx0000001T0zk

    </partner>
    <rest>http://na1.salesforce.com/services/data/v{version}/
    </rest>

<sobjects>http://na1.salesforce.com/services/data/v{version}/sobjects/

    </sobjects>
    <search>http://na1.salesforce.com/services/data/v{version}/search/

    </search>
    <query>http://na1.salesforce.com/services/data/v{version}/query/
    </query>
    <profile>http://na1.salesforce.com/005x0000001S2b9
    </profile>
</urls>
<active>true</active>
<user_type>STANDARD</user_type>
<language>en_US</language>
<locale>en_US</locale>
<utcOffset>-28800000</utcOffset>
<last_modified_date>2010-06-28T20:54:09.000Z</last_modified_date>
</user>
```

The following is a response in JSON format:

```
{"id":"http://na1.salesforce.com/id/00Dx0000001T0zk/005x0000001S2b9",
"asserted_user":true,
"user_id":"005x0000001S2b9",
"organization_id":"00Dx0000001T0zk",
"nick_name":"admin1.27775/8168398293E12foofoofoofoo",
"display_name":"Alan Van",
"email":"admin@2060747062579699.com",
"status":{"created_date":null,"body":null},
"photos":{"picture":"http://na1.salesforce.com/profilephoto/005/F",
   "thumbnail":"http://na1.salesforce.com/profilephoto/005/T"},
"urls":

{"enterprise":"http://na1.salesforce.com/services/Soap/c/{version}/00Dx0000001T0zk",


"metadata":"http://na1.salesforce.com/services/Soap/m/{version}/00Dx0000001T0zk",


"partner":"http://na1.salesforce.com/services/Soap/u/{version}/00Dx0000001T0zk",

   "rest":"http://na1.salesforce.com/services/data/v{version}/",

"sobjects":"http://na1.salesforce.com/services/data/v{version}/sobjects/",


"search":"http://na1.salesforce.com/services/data/v{version}/search/",

   "query":"http://na1.salesforce.com/services/data/v{version}/query/",

   "profile":"http://na1.salesforce.com/005x0000001S2b9"},
"active":true,
"user_type":"STANDARD",
"language":"en_US",
"locale":"en_US",
"utcOffset":-28800000,
"last_modified_date":"2010-06-28T20:54:09.000+0000"}
```

After making an invalid request, the following are possible responses from Salesforce:

Request Problem	Error Code
HTTP	403 (forbidden) — HTTPS_Required
Missing access token	403 (forbidden) — Missing_OAuth_Token
Invalid access token	403 (forbidden) — Bad_OAuth_Token
Users in a different organization	403 (forbidden) — Wrong_Org
Invalid or bad user or organization ID	404 (not found) — Bad_Id
Deactivated user or inactive organization	404 (not found) — Inactive

Request Problem	Error Code
User lacks proper access to organization or information	404 (not found) — No_Access
Request to the endpoint of a site	404 (not found) — No_Site_Endpoint
Invalid version	406 (not acceptable) — Invalid_Version
Invalid callback	406 (not acceptable) — Invalid_Callback

Revoking OAuth Tokens

When a user logs out of an app, or the app times out or in other ways becomes invalid, the logged-in users' credentials are cleared from the mobile app. This effectively ends the connection to the server, but you can also explicitly revoke the token on the server.

When users request their data from within the external application (the consumer's page), they are authenticated. You can revoke their access tokens, or the refresh token and all related access tokens, using revocation. Developers can use this feature when configuring a Log Out button in their application.

Revoking Tokens

To revoke OAuth 2.0 tokens, use the revocation endpoint:

```
https://login.salesforce.com/services/oauth2/revoke
```

Construct a POST request that includes the following parameters using the `application/x-www-form-urlencoded` format in the HTTP request entity-body. For example:

```
POST /revoke HTTP/1.1
Host: https://login.salesforce.com/services/oauth2/revoke
Content-Type: application/x-www-form-urlencoded

token=currenttoken
```

If an access token is included, we invalidate it and revoke the token. If a refresh token is included, we revoke it as well as any associated access tokens.

The authorization server indicates successful processing of the request by returning an HTTP status code 200. For all error conditions, a status code 400 is used along with one of the following error responses.

- `unsupported_token_type`—token type not supported

- `invalid_token`—the token was invalid

For Sandbox, use `test.salesforce.com` instead of `login.salesforce.com`.

Creating a Remote Access Application

Before a mobile device can connect with the service, you need to create a remote access application. The remote access application includes a Consumer Key, a prerequisite to all development scenarios in this guide.

1. Log into your Database.com or Force.com instance.
2. Navigate to **App Setup** > **Develop** > **Remote Access**.
3. Click **New**.
4. For `Application`, enter a name, such as `Test Client`
5. For `Callback URL`, enter `sfdc://success`

 Note: The `Callback URL` does not have to be a valid URL; it only has to match what the app expects in this field. You can use any custom prefix, such as `sfdc:///`.

6. For `Email`, enter your email address.
7. Click **Save**.

 Tip: The detail page for your remote access configuration displays a consumer key. It's a good idea to copy the key, as you'll need it later. Mobile apps do not use the **Consumer Secret**, so you can just ignore this value.

Remote Access

« Back to List: Remote Access

Printable View | Help for this Page

Remote Access Detail   [Edit] [Delete]

Basic Information

		= Required Information
Application	My Hybrid App	
Description	Demo of the Salesforce Mobile SDK.	
Logo Image URL	https://example.com/images/logo.png	
Info URL	https://example.com/hybridapp/info.html	
Contact Phone		
Contact Email	user@example.com	

Integration

		= Required Information
Callback URL	https://login.salesforce.com/services/oauth2/success	

Policies

		= Required Information
No user approval required for users in this organization	[i]	

Authentication

		= Required Information
My App uses digital signatures for login		
Consumer Key	3MVG9Km_cBLhsuPzTtcGHsZpj9Bzs2Uk4MI6eW8YPP_I3Uwrld56s15QBgRkrY5y8BpMqU1XUk2LgZGx6xo79	
Consumer Secret	Click to reveal	
Created Date	5/30/2012 8:42 AM	Created By Andy Admin

Connected Apps

A Connected App is an application that can connect to salesforce.com over Identity and Data APIs. Connected Apps use the standard OAuth 2.0 protocol to authenticate, provide Single Sign-On, and acquire access tokens for use with Salesforce APIs. In addition to standard OAuth capabilities, Connected Apps add additional levels of control, allowing administrators explicit control over who may use the application, and various security policies which should be enforced.

Connected Apps are enabled in all new Developer Edition organizations. Existing Developer Edition organizations and all other Salesforce organizations can request to have Connected Apps enabled as part of a pilot program.

 Note: The Connected Apps feature is currently available through a pilot program. For information on enabling it for your organization, contact your salesforce.com representative. Any unreleased services or features referenced in this or other press releases or public statements are not currently available and might not be delivered on time or at all. Customers who purchase our services should make their purchase decisions based upon features that are currently available.

Developing and Managing Connected Apps

Connected Apps begin with a developer defining OAuth metadata about the application, including:

- Basic descriptive and contact information for the Connected App
- The OAuth scopes and callback URL for the Connected App
- Optional IP ranges where the Connected App might be running
- Optional information about mobile policies the Connected App can enforce

In return, the developer is provided an OAuth client Id and client secret, as well as an install URL for the Connected App. The developer can then provide this URL to a Salesforce administrator.

The administrator can install the Connected App into their organization and use profiles, permission sets, and IP range restrictions to control which users can access the application. Management is done from a detail page for the Connected App. The administrator can also uninstall the Connected App and install a newer version. When the app is updated, the developer can notify administrators that there is a new version available for the app — their existing installation URL installs the new version.

Developer Tasks

The lifecycle of a Connected App is made up of these steps:

- Creating a Connected App
- Publishing a Connected App
- Deleting a Connected App
- Updating a Connected App

Creating a Connected App

Create a Connected App by doing the following:

1. Click **Your Name** > **Setup** > **Create** > **Apps**.
2. In the Connected Apps section, click **New**.

Apps

Help for this Page

An *app* is a group of tabs that work as a unit to provide functionality. Users can switch between apps using the Force.com app drop-down menu at the top-right corner of every page.

You can customize existing apps to match the way you work, or build new apps by grouping standard and custom tabs.

ⓘ Custom apps work in conjunction with User Profile Tab Visibility settings. View User Profiles now.

Apps   Quick Start | New | Reorder   Apps Help ?

Action   App Label   Service Cloud Console Custom Description

Connected Apps   New

No Apps found.

The information required to create a Connected App is divided into these parts:

- Basic Information describes your application, its appearance in the list of available applications, and how someone can contact you about the application.
- API Integration specifies how your application communicates with Salesforce.
- Mobile Integration specifies PIN length and session timeout values available for mobile applications.
- IP Ranges are the list of IP addresses that can access the app without requiring the user to authenticate. You set these after creating the app.

When you've finished entering the information, click **Save** to save your new app. You can now publish your app, make further edits, or delete it. Saving your app gives you the Consumer Key and Consumer Secret the app uses to communicate with Salesforce.

Connected App Basic Information

Specify basic information about your app in this section, including the app name, logo, and contact information.

1. For **Connected App Name**, enter the name for your application. This name displays in the list of Connected Apps.

   Note: The name must be completely unique in your organization. You can't reuse an existing name or the name of a deleted Connected App.

2. In **Description**, enter an optional description for your application. This also displays in the list of Connected Apps.

3. Optionally enter the **Logo Image URL** for your application logo. The URL must use HTTPS and the logo cannot be larger than 125 pixels high or 200 pixels wide. The default logo is a cloud.

4. You can optionally enter an **Info URL** if you have a Web page for more information about your application.

5. Enter a phone number in **Contact Phone** for salesforce.com to use in case we need to contact you. This number is not provided to administrators installing the app.

6. In **Contact Email**, enter the email address salesforce.com should use for contacting you or your support team. This address is not provided to administrators installing the app.

▼ Basic Information	
Connected App Name	ExampleConnApp
Description	Demonstrate Connected App creation.
Logo Image URL	
Info URL	http://www.connapp.com
Contact Phone	415-555-1234
Contact Email	Support@ConnApp.com

Connected App API Integration

The API Integration section controls how your app communicates with Salesforce.

1. Enter a **Callback URL**. This is the URL (endpoint) that Salesforce calls back to your application during OAuth; it's the OAuth `redirect_uri`.

2. Check **Use Digital Signatures** if the app uses a certificate.

3. Pick the **Selected OAuth Scopes** for your application from the list of available OAuth scopes. The scopes refer to permissions given by the user running the Connected App:

   • Access and manage your Chatter feed (with the Chatter REST API)
   • Access and manage your data
   • Access your basic information
   • Full access
   • Perform requests on your behalf at any time
   • Provide access to custom applications
   • Provide access to your data via the Web

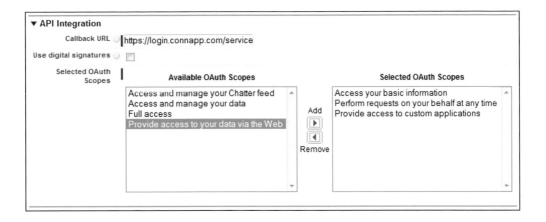

If your organization had the `No user approval required for users in this organization` option selected on your remote access prior to the Spring '12 release, users in the same organization as the one the app was created in still have automatic approval for the app. The read-only `No user approval required for users in this organization` checkbox is selected to show this condition. For Connected Apps, the recommended procedure after you've created an app is for administrators to install the app and then set `Permitted Users` to `Admin-approved users`. If the remote access option was not checked originally, the checkbox doesn't display.

Connected App Mobile Integration

If your app is a mobile application, you might wish to enforce policies for Screen Locking and Pin Protection. These policies are automatically enforced by the Salesforce Mobile SDK (`http://developer.force.com/mobilesdk`) or you can implement this manually by reading the `mobile_policies` object from the user's Identity URL. If you enforce this, check **Implements Screen Locking & Pin Protection** to give an administrator the option of setting the session timeout and PIN length for mobile applications after installing the Connected App.

Connected App IP Ranges

After you've created the app, you can specify IP ranges by clicking **New** at IP Ranges. These IP ranges act as a requested whitelist of acceptable IP addresses that can access the app. Enter a valid IP address in the **Start IP Address** field and a higher IP address in the **End IP Address** field. You can enter multiple, discontinuous ranges by clicking **New** to enter each range. Once the app is installed, each organization's administrator can approve or bypass the ranges by setting IP restrictions.

Publishing a Connected App

After creating a Connected App, publish it to make it available to other users. An app that has never been published appears in the Connected Apps list with Unpublished Changes status. Clicking the **Connected App Name** in the list opens the editing page for the app.

You can perform the following tasks:

- **Publish** creates an installation URL for the app.
- **Edit** lets you make changes to the app information you specify when creating the app.
- **Delete** removes the app completely, though the name is remembered and cannot be reused.

When you click **Publish,** you are asked to confirm that you want to publish the Connected App. Confirm by clicking **Publish**. The **Version** is incremented by 1 and new values are created:

- **Installation URL** – Administrators use this URL to install the Connected App in their organizations.
- **Consumer Key** – A value used by the consumer to identify itself to Salesforce. Referred to as `client_id` in OAuth 2.0.
- **Consumer Secret** – A secret used by the consumer to establish ownership of the consumer key. Referred to as `client_secret` in OAuth 2.0.

Note: Any OAuth approvals done for an unpublished Connected App, for example during testing, will be valid against the first published version as well. The approvals will not transfer to subsequently published versions.

Deleting a Connected App

To delete a Connected App, click the **Connected App Name** in the list of apps. Click **Delete** on the editing page and confirm by clicking **Delete** again. Even though the app is removed from your list, you cannot reuse the app name.

If you delete a Connected App that has been installed in an organization, the organization administrator still sees the app in the Connected Apps list, but they cannot run the app and the only action available to them is **Remove**.

Updating a Connected App

You can update a Connected App at any time. Clicking the **Connected App Name** in the list opens the editing page for the app. Click **New Version** to bring up the edit page where you can make changes. Save your changes by clicking **Save**. If you return to the list of Connected Apps now, you'll see your app shown with the Unpublished Changes status. Click the app name and click **Publish** on the editing screen to publish the app. Publishing the app makes any earlier version unavailable.

Administrator Tasks

Administrators perform these tasks with Connected Apps:

- Installing a Connected App
- Managing a Connected App
- Uninstalling a Connected App
- Upgrading a Connected App

Installing a Connected App

You install a Connected App with the installation URL provided by the Connected App developer. The easiest way to install the app in your organization is to log into your Salesforce organization and then paste the URL into your browser to start the installation process. You'll see a confirmation screen with the app name, its description, and information about how to control user access to the app after it's installed. Click **Install** to complete the installation.

If you are logged into more than one Salesforce organization, the installation will select one. Check the **username** shown in the upper right corner to make sure that the app will be installed in the correct organization. If the **username** shown isn't the correct one, click **Not you?** to log out and stop the installation.

If any version of the Connected App is already installed in your organization you'll see an error message telling you this. Uninstall your current version and then install the new version.

After installing a Connected App, you're shown the detail page for the app. You can edit the app policies from this page.

Managing a Connected App

Connected Apps are managed through the editing page. You can find your app under *Your Name* > **Setup** > **Manage Apps** > **Connected Apps**. You can edit, uninstall, and review information about the app from this page.

- Click `Edit` to make changes to the app on the Edit page.

  `App Policies` are available for every Connected App.

  ◊ `Permitted Users` determines who can run the app.

    - `All Users`, the default, allows anyone in the organization to self-authorize the app. This means each user has to approve the app the first time they access it. If you switch from `All Users` to `Admin-approved users`, anyone currently using the app loses their access unless they belong to a permission set you have specified for the app.
    - `Admin-approved users` limits access to those users with the permission set or sets specified, but these users don't need to approve the app before they can access it. You manage permission sets for the app from the Detail page.

  ◊ `IP Restrictions` refers to the IP restrictions that the users of this Connected App are subject to. An administrator can choose to either enforce or bypass these restrictions by choosing one of the following options.

    - `Enforce IP Restrictions` – Default. A user running this app is subject to the organization's IP restrictions, such as IP ranges set in the user's profile.
    - `Relax IP Restrictions with Second Factor` – A user running this app bypasses the organization's IP restrictions if either of these conditions are true:

      - The app has IP ranges whitelisted and is using the Web server OAuth authentication flow. Only requests coming from the whitelisted IPs are allowed.

- The app has no IP range whitelist, is using the Web server or user-agent OAuth authentication flow, and the user successfully completes Identity Confirmation.

- `Relax IP Restrictions` – A user running this app is not subject to any IP restrictions.

◊ `Start URL` is used if the Connected App uses single sign-on. In this case, set the URL to the page the user goes to to start the authentication process.

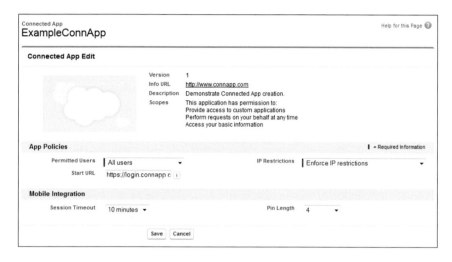

This location will also appear in the application switcher menu.

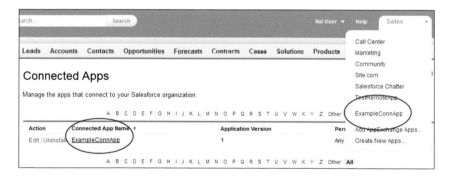

◊ `Mobile Integration` settings are available for any Connected App that's a mobile application.

- `Session Timeout` specifies how much time can pass while the app is idle before the app locks itself and requires the PIN before continuing. Allowable values are 1, 5, 10, and 30 minutes.

- `Pin Length` sets the length of the identification number sent for authentication confirmation. The length can be from 4 to 8 digits, inclusive.

- Uninstall the Connected App by clicking `Uninstall`. Click `OK` to confirm the uninstallation. You have to uninstall an app before you can install a new version.
- Click the app's name to review the Connected App on the Detail page. You can click `Edit` or `Uninstall` from this page to make changes after reviewing the app. This is also where you assign profiles and permission sets to the app.

  ◊ Click `Manage Permission Sets` to select the permission sets for the profiles for this app from the Application Permission Set Assignment page. Select the permission sets to have access to the app.

  ◊ Click `Manage Profiles` to select the profiles for this app from the Application Profile Assignment page. Select the profiles to have access to the app.

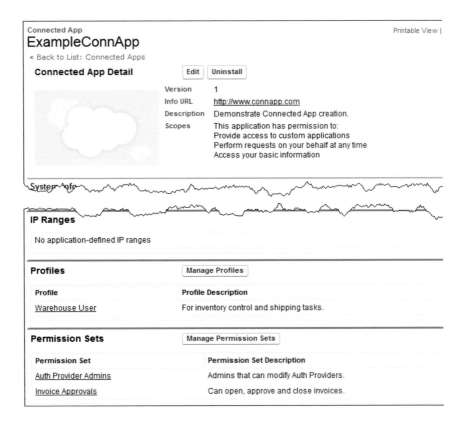

Only the users belonging to at least one of the selected profiles or permission sets can run the app if you have selected `Admin-approved users` for the `Permitted Users` value. If you selected `All Users` instead, profiles and permission sets are ignored.

- If the app has been deleted by its developer, `Remove` is the only action available, and removes the app from the list.

About PIN Security

Mobile Connected Apps have an additional layer of security via PIN protection on the app. This PIN protection is for the mobile app itself, and isn't the same as the PIN protection on the device or the login security provided by the Salesforce organization.

In order to use PIN protection, the developer must select the **Implements Screen Locking & Pin Protection** checkbox when creating the Connected App. Mobile app administrators then have the option of enforcing PIN protection and customizing timeout duration and PIN length.

> **Note:** Because PIN security is implemented in the mobile device's operating system, only native and hybrid mobile apps can use PIN protection; HTML5 Web apps can't use PIN protection.

In practice, PIN protection can be used so that the mobile app locks up if it isn't used for a specified number of minutes. Note that when a mobile app is sent to the background, the clock continues to tick.

To illustrate how PIN protection works:

1. User turns on phone and enters PIN for the device.
2. User starts mobile app (Connected App).
3. User enters login information for Salesforce organization.
4. User enters PIN code for mobile app.
5. User works in the app, and then sends it to the background by opening another app (or receiving a call, etc.).
6. The mobile app times out.
7. User re-opens the app, and the app PIN screen displays (for the mobile app, not the device).
8. User enters app PIN, and can resume working.

Uninstalling a Connected App

Uninstall a Connected App by clicking **Uninstall** next to the app name at *Your Name* > **Setup** > **Manage Apps** > **Connected Apps**. Click **OK** in the confirmation window.

> **Note:** When a Connected App is uninstalled, the access and refresh tokens of all users of the application are removed. This prevents a user from running the application later, using an existing access token, without explicitly approving the application themselves.

Upgrading a Connected App

When a new version becomes available for an installed Connected App, you must uninstall the current version before you can install the new one. Use the same Installation URL you used previously to install the app.

Connected App Error Codes

A user might see the following error code when trying to use a Connected App.

Fault Code	Error	Notes
1805	APP_ACCESS_DENIED	The user doesn't have administrator approval to access this Connected App.

Chapter 4

Native iOS Development

The two main things the iOS native SDK provides:

- Automate the OAuth2 login process and make it easy to integrate this with your app.
- Access to the REST API with all the infrastructure classes (including third-party libraries such as RestKit) for making that access as easy as possible.

When you create a new project using the Salesforce Mobile SDK, a template application is included automatically. This simple app allows you to connect to a organization and run a simple query. It doesn't do much, but it lets you know things are working as designed, and gives you the foundation of your own app.

iOS Native Quick Start

Use the following procedure to get started quickly.

1. Make sure you meet all of the native iOS requirements.
2. Install the Mobile SDK for iOS.
3. Run the template app.

Native iOS Requirements

- XCode—4.0 is the minimum, we recommend the latest version.
- iOS 4.3 (soon 5.0)
- Install the Mobile SDK.
- A Developer Edition organization with a remote access application.

Installing the Mobile SDK for iOS

1. In your browser, navigate to the Mobile SDK iOS GitHub repository:
   `https://github.com/forcedotcom/SalesforceMobileSDK-iOS.`
2. Clone the repository to your local file system by issuing the following command:
   `git clone`
   `git://github.com/forcedotcom/SalesforceMobileSDK-iOS.git`

    Note: If you have the GitHub app for Mac OS X, click **Clone in Mac**.

3. Open the OS X Terminal app in the directory where you installed the cloned repository and run the install script from the command line: `./install.sh`
4. You also need to download the sample app from GitHub:
   `https://github.com/forcedotcom/SalesforceMobileSDK-Samples/tree/master/iOS/CloudTunesNative`

Creating a New Native iOS App in Xcode

Use the following procedure to create and configure a new Force.com–based Application project.

1. Open Xcode and create a new project (Shift-Command-N).

2. Select **Native Force.com REST App** and click **Next**.

3. In the `Choose options for your new project` dialog, enter `NativeTestApp`.

> **Note:** You might also need to enter a Company Identifier prefix if you haven't used Xcode before.

4. Make sure the checkbox for **Use Automatic Reference Counting** is cleared.

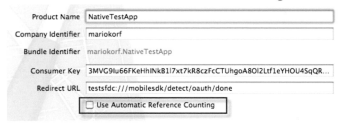

Product Name	NativeTestApp
Company Identifier	mariokorf
Bundle Identifier	mariokorf.NativeTestApp
Consumer Key	3MVG9Iu66FKeHhINkB1I7xt7kR8czFcCTUhgoA8OI2Ltf1eYHOU4SqQR...
Redirect URL	testsfdc:///mobilesdk/detect/oauth/done
	☐ Use Automatic Reference Counting

5. Click **Next**.

6. Specify a location for your new project and click **Create**.

Running the Xcode Project Template App

The Xcode project template includes a sample application you can run right away.

1. Press **Command-R** and the default template app builds and then runs in the iOS simulator.

> **Note:** If you get build errors, make sure **Automatic Reference Counting (ARC)** is turned off.

   a. Select your project in the Navigator.

   b. In the Build Settings tab, toggle the `Objective-C Automatic Reference Counting` value to `No`.

2. On startup, the application starts the OAuth authentication flow, which results in an authentication page. Enter your credentials, and click **Login**.

3. Tap **Allow** when asked for permission

You should now be able to compile and run the sample project. It's a simple app that logs you into an org via OAuth2, issues a `'select Name from User'` query, and displays the result in a `UITableView`.

Using the Mobile SDK in an Existing Project

If you want to incorporate the Mobile SDK into an existing iOS project, do the following.

1. In Xcode, drag the folder `native/dependencies` into your project (select **Create groups** for any added folders).
2. Open the **Build Settings** tab for the project and set `Other Linker Flags` to `-ObjC -all_load`.
3. Open the **Build Phases** tab for the project main target and link against the following required frameworks:

   - `CFNetwork.framework`
   - `CoreData.framework`
   - `MobileCoreServices.framework`
   - `SystemConfiguration.framework`
   - `Security.framework`
   - `libxml2.dylib`

4. Import the `SalesforceSDK` header via `#import "SFRestAPI.h"`.
5. Build the project to verify that the installation is successful.
6. Refer to the SFRestAPI documentation for some sample code to log into a Salesforce instance and issue a REST API call.

iOS RestAPIExplorer Sample Application

The Xcode Project Template is itself a sample application, but it only does one thing: issue a SOQL query and return a result. The RestAPIExplorer sample app has a lot more functionality you can examine and work into your own apps.

The RestAPIExplorer sample app is in the Mobile SDK for iOS under `native/SampleApps/RestAPIExplorer`.

Chapter 5

Native Android Development

The two main things the Android native SDK provides are:

- Automation of the OAuth2 login process, making it easy to integrate the process with your app.
- Access to the REST API, with infrastructure classes that simplify that access.

The Android Salesforce Mobile SDK includes several sample native applications. We also provide an ant target to quickly create a new application.

Android Native Quick Start

Use the following procedure to get started quickly.

1. Make sure you meet all of the native Android requirements.
2. Install the Mobile SDK for Android.
3. At the command line, run an ant script to create a new Android project , and then run the template application from the command line.

Native Android Requirements

- Java JDK 6.
- Apache Ant 1.8 or later.
- Android SDK, version 20 or later—`http://developer.android.com/sdk/installing.html`.

 Note: For best results, install all previous versions of the Android SDK as well as your target version.

- Eclipse 3.6 or later. See `http://developer.android.com/sdk/requirements.html` for other versions.
- Android ADT (Android Development Tools) plugin for Eclipse, version 20 or later—`http://developer.android.com/sdk/eclipse-adt.html#installing`.
- In order to run the application in the Emulator, you need to set up at least one Android Virtual Device (AVD) that targets Platform 2.2 or above (we recommend 2.2). To learn how to set up an AVD in Eclipse, follow the instructions at `http://developer.android.com/guide/developing/devices/managing-avds.html`.
- A Developer Edition organization with a remote access application.

The `SalesforceSDK` project is built with the Android 3.0 (Honeycomb) library. The primary reason for this is that we want to be able to make a conditional check at runtime for file system encryption capabilities. This check is bypassed on earlier Android platforms; thus, you can still use the `salesforcesdk.jar` in earlier Android application versions, down to the mininum-supported Android 2.2.

Installing the Mobile SDK for Android

1. In your browser, navigate to the Mobile SDK Android GitHub repository: https://github.com/forcedotcom/SalesforceMobileSDK-Android.
2. Clone the repository to your local file system by issuing the following command:
   `git clone`
   `git://github.com/forcedotcom/SalesforceMobileSDK-Android.git`
3. Open a command prompt in the directory where you installed the cloned repository, and run the install script from the command line: `./install.sh`

    Note: Windows users run `cscript install.vbs`.

Create shell variables:

1. `ANDROID_SDK_DIR` pointing to the Android SDK directory
2. `SALESFORCE_SDK_DIR` pointing to your clone of the Salesforce Mobile SDK repository, for example: `/home/jon/SalesforceMobileSDK-Android`.
3. `NATIVE_DIR` pointing to `$SALESFORCE_SDK_DIR/native`
4. `TARGET_DIR` pointing to a location you've defined to contain your Android project.

 Note: If you haven't set up these variables, make sure to replace `$ANDROID_SDK_DIR`, `$SALESFORCE_SDK_DIR`, `$NATIVE_DIR` and `$TARGET_DIR` in the various code snippets in this guide with the actual paths.

Creating a New Android Project

We've made it easy to create a native Android project by using an ant script. You'll need to provide the following parameters when you run the script.

- `appName` — the name for the new application
- `targetDir` — the directory where the code should reside (the same as `$TARGET_DIR` if you defined that environment variable)
- `packageName` — the Java package for the new application, for example, `com.acme.mobileapp`.

To create a native Android project:

1. Open a command prompt in the location where you installed the SDK (or `$SALESFORCE_SDK_DIR` if you created that variable).

2. Enter `ant create_native -Dapp.name={appName}`
   `-Dtarget.dir={targetDir} -Dpackage.name={packageName}`

The Android project contains a simple application you can build and run.

Android Template Application

The template native app for Android allows you to login and do standard CRM tasks, such as queries and inserts.

To build the new application, do the following:

1. In a text editor, open `$TARGET_DIR/res/values/rest.xml`.
2. Enter your OAuth client ID and callback URL, and then save the file.
3. Open a command prompt and enter the following commands:

```
cd $TARGET_DIR
$ANDROID_SDK_DIR/tools/android update project -p . -t 1
ant clean debug
```

 Note: The `-t 1` parameter specifies Android 11 as the target Android version. For a list of target IDs, use `android.bat list targets`.

4. If your emulator is not running, use the Android AVD Manager to start it. If you are using a real device, connect it.
5. Enter `ant installd`.

Setting Up Projects in Eclipse

The repository you cloned has other sample apps you can run. To import those into Eclipse:

1. Launch Eclipse and select `$TARGET_DIR` as your workspace directory.
2. Select **Window** > **Preferences**, choose the **Android** section, and enter the the Android SDK location.
3. Click OK.
4. Select **File** > **Import** and select **General** > **Existing Projects into Workspace**.
5. Click Next.
6. Select `$NATIVE_DIR` as your root directory and import the projects listed in Android Project Files.

7. In the navigator, right-click SalesforceSDKTest, choose **New** > **Folder**, and set the folder name to gen. If the folder already exists, click Cancel.

8. In the same way, create a gen folder for RestExplorer and RestExplorerTest projects.

9. Right–click the SalesforceSDK project and create a folder called res.

Android Project Files

Inside the $NATIVE_DIR, you will find several projects:

1. SalesforceSDK —The SalesforceSDK, which provides support for OAuth2 and REST API calls

2. SalesforceSDKTest —Tests for the SalesforceSDK project

3. TemplateApp — Template used when creating new native applications using SalesforceSDK

4. TemplateAppTest — Tests for the Templateapp project.

5. RestExplorer — App using SalesforceSDK to explore the REST API calls

6. RestExplorerTest —Tests for the RestExplorer project

7. SampleApps/CloudTunes — A sample native application using SalesforceSDK, used in the Mobile SDK Workbook

Cleaning and Building From Eclipse

Depending on the Android SDK Tools version you use, you might experience problems around cleaning your workspace (**Project** > **Clean**). Specifically, projects that are dependent on Android Library projects might not properly follow the build dependency ordering, so when every project is cleaned, dependent projects do not pick up the existence of the Library project. The result is that all of the non-Library projects will have build errors after a clean.

If you would like to rebuild everything, we recommend cleaning/rebuilding the Library (SalesforceSDK) project by itself first, followed by cleaning and rebuilding the dependent projects.

Android RestExplorer Sample Application

The RestExplorer is a sample app that demonstrates how to use the OAuth and REST API functions of the SalesforceSDK. It is also useful to investigate the various REST API actions from a Honeycomb tablet.

1. To run the application, right-click the **RestExplorer** project and choose **Run As > Android Application**.
2. To run the tests, right-click the **RestExplorerTest** project and choose **Run As > Android JUnit Test**.

Chapter 6

Hybrid Development

Hybrid apps combine the ease of HTML5 Web app development with the power and features of the native platform.

Hybrid apps depend on HTML and JavaScript files. These files can be stored on the device or on the server.

- **Device** — Hybrid apps developed with `forcetk` JavaScript library wrap a Web app inside the Salesforce Mobile Container. In this methodology, the JavaScript and HTML files are stored on the device.
- **Salesforce Mobile Container** — Hybrid apps developed using Visualforce technology store the HTML and JavaScript files on the server and are delivered through the native container.

Hybrid Apps Quick Start

Use the following procedure to get started quickly.

1. Make sure you meet all of the Hybrid Apps Requirements on page 58.
2. Install the Mobile SDK.

   - Installing the Mobile SDK for iOS on page 48
   - Installing the Mobile SDK for Android on page 53

3. Create a Remote Access Application on page 33.

    Note: When filling in the details for the Callback URL:

   - For iOS use
     `https://login.salesforce.com/services/oauth2/success`
   - For Android use `myapp:///mobilesdk/detect/oauth/done`,
     where `myapp` is specific to your application

4. Run the Sample App on page 60.

When you're done with the sample app you can add more functionality.

1. Create a Mobile Page to List Information on page 64
2. Create a Mobile Page for Detailed Information on page 68
3. Customize the Hybrid Sample App to Use the Camera on page 118

Hybrid Apps Requirements

For all target devices, you will need:

- Ant 1.8.0 or later
- Git - see these helpful instructions http://help.github.com/set-up-git-redirect.

If you are developing apps for iOS devices, you will also need **Xcode 4.2 or above**.

If you are developing apps for Android devices, you will also need:

- Eclipse Classic
- Android SDK (r20 or above)
- ADT Plugin (r20 or above)

Creating a Hybrid App Project for iOS

To create a new project:

1. In Xcode, create a new "Hybrid Force.com App" project (Command-Shift-N in Xcode). These parameters are required.

    *   **Consumer Public Key**: The Consumer Key from your Remote Access app.
    *   **OAuth Redirect URL**: The Callback URL from your Remote Access app.
    *   **Company Identifier**: Something like com.mycompany.foo - this should correspond with an App ID you created in your Apple iOS dev center account.
    *   Use Automatic Reference Counting: Uncheck.

At the time of writing, there is a bug in the Hybrid Force.com App template that causes the app to be incorrectly packaged. If you try to run the app, it will fail with *"ERROR: Start Page at 'www/bootstrap.html' was not found"* in the output console in Xcode.

To fix this:

1. Right-click the yellow www folder and delete it by clicking **Delete, Remove References Only**.
2. Right-click your project folder, select **Add Files to "*My Project*"** and navigate to the www directory inside the project directory.

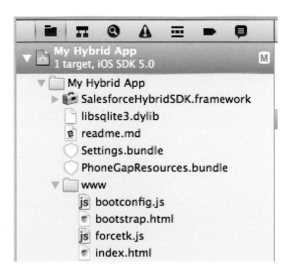

3. Ensure that **Create folder references for any added folders** is selected, then click **Add**. Notice that the www folder is now shown in blue.

Now the app will run correctly.

Creating a Hybrid Project for Android

To create the project:

1. In Eclipse, select **File** > **Import** > **General** > **Existing Projects into Workspace**.
2. Locate the sample **ContactExplorer** project:
   `SalesforceMobileSDK-Android/hybrid/SampleApps/ContactExplorer` and select it as the root directory. Ensure that **Copy projects into workspace** is selected, and click **Finish**.
3. To avoid confusion with the standard ContactExplorer sample, right-click the ContactExplorer project and rename it. Open `res/values/strings.xml`, and edit `app_name` to match the new project name.
4. To configure your app with its Remote Access parameters, open `assets/www/bootconfig.js` and edit the following values:

   - `remoteAccessConsumerKey`: The Consumer Key from your Remote Access app.
   - `oauthRedirectURI`: The Callback URL from your Remote Access app.

5. You will need to create an Android Virtual Device, if you have not already done so. In Eclipse, select **Window** > **AVD Manager** and click **New**. You can enable camera support in the device if you wish.

Running the Sample Hybrid App

You should now be able to compile and run the sample project, either on the simulator or a physical device. In both environments, you can select either a connected physical device or a simulator on which to run the app. If you're using an iOS device, you must configure a profile as described in the Xcode 4 User Guide. Similarly, Android devices must be set up as described in the Android developer documentation.

Whichever way you run the app, after showing an initial 'splash screen', you should see the Salesforce login screen.

Log in with your DE username and password, and you will be prompted to allow your app access to your data in Salesforce.

Tap **Allow** and you should be able to retrieve lists of contacts and accounts from your DE account.

Tap to retrieve Contact and Account records from your DE account.

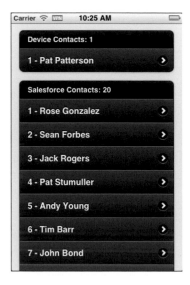

Notice the app can also retrieve contacts from the device - something that an equivalent web app would be unable to do. Let's take a closer look at how the app can do this.

How the Sample App Works

After completing the login process, the sample app displays `index.html` (located in the www folder). When the page has completed loading and the mobile framework is ready, the `onDeviceReady()` function calls `regLinkClickHandlers()` (in `inline.js`). `regLinkClickHandlers()` sets up five click handlers for the various functions in the sample app.

```
$j('#link_fetch_device_contacts').click(function() {
    SFHybridApp.logToConsole("link_fetch_device_contacts clicked");
    var options = new ContactFindOptions();
    options.filter = ""; // empty search string returns all contacts
    options.multiple = true;
    var fields = ["name"];
    navigator.contacts.find(fields, onSuccessDevice,
        onErrorDevice, options);
});
```

This handler calls `find()` on the `navigator.contacts` object to retrieve the contact list from the device. The `onSuccessDevice()` function renders the contact list into the `index.html` page.

```
$j('#link_fetch_sfdc_contacts').click(function() {
    SFHybridApp.logToConsole("link_fetch_sfdc_contacts clicked");
    forcetkClient.query("SELECT Name FROM Contact",
        onSuccessSfdcContacts, onErrorSfdc);
});
```

The `#link_fetch_sfdc_contacts` handler runs a query using the `forcetkClient` object. This object is set up during the initial OAuth 2.0 interaction, and gives access to the Force.com REST API in the context of the authenticated user. Here we retrieve the names of all the contacts in the DE account and `onSuccessSfdcContacts()` renders them as a list on the `index.html` page.

```
$j('#link_fetch_sfdc_accounts').click(function() {
    SFHybridApp.logToConsole("link_fetch_sfdc_accounts clicked");
    forcetkClient.query("SELECT Name FROM Account",
        onSuccessSfdcAccounts, onErrorSfdc);
});
```

The `#link_fetch_sfdc_accounts` handler is very similar to the previous one, fetching Account records via the Force.com REST API. The remaining handlers, `#link_reset` and `#link_logout`, clear the displayed lists and log out the user respectively.

Create a Mobile Page to List Information

The sample hybrid app is useful in many respects, and serves as a good starting point to learn hybrid mobile app development. In this tutorial, you modify the sample hybrid mobile app to display Merchandise records in the custom Warehouse app schema.

You can build the Warehouse schema quickly using the getting started content online: `http://wiki.developerforce.com/page/Developing_Cloud_Apps_-_Coding_Optional`.

Modify the App's Initialization Block (index.html)

In this section, you modify the view file (`index.html`) and the controller (`inline.js`) to make the app specific to the Warehouse schema and display all records in the Merchandise custom object.

In your app, you want a list of Merchandise records to appear on the default Home page of the mobile app. Consequently, the first thing to do is to modify what happens automatically when the app calls the `onDeviceReady` function. Add the following code to the tail end of the sample `salesforceSessionRefreshed` function in `index.html`.

```
// log message
SFHybridApp.logToConsole("Calling out for records");
// register click event handlers -- see inline.js
regLinkClickHandlers();
// retrieve Merchandise records, including the Id for links
forcetkClient.query("SELECT Id, Name, Price__c, Quantity__c
    FROM Merchandise__c", onSuccessSfdcMerchandise, onErrorSfdc);
```

Notice that this JavaScript code leverages the `forcetk` library to query the Force.com database with a basic SOQL statement and retrieve all records from the Merchandise custom object. On success, the function calls the JavaScript function `onSuccessSfdcMerchandise` (which you build in a moment).

Create the App's mainpage View (index.html)

To display the Merchandise records in a standard mobile, touch-oriented user interface, scroll down in `index.html` and replace the entire `<body>` tag with the following HTML.

```
<!-- Main page, to display list of Merchandise once app starts -->
<div data-role="page" data-theme="b" id="mainpage">
   <!-- page header -->
   <div data-role="header">
      <!-- button for logging out -->
      <a href='#' id="link_logout" data-role="button"
         data-icon='delete'>
            Log Out
      </a>
```

```
      <!-- page title -->
      <h2>List</h2>
   </div>
   <!-- page content -->
   <div id="#content" data-role="content">
      <!-- page title -->
      <h2>Mobile Inventory</h2>
      <!-- list of merchandise, links to detail pages -->
      <div id="div_merchandise_list">
      <!-- built dynamically by function onSuccessSfdcMerchandise -->

      </div>
   </div>
</div>
```

Overall, notice that the updated view uses standard HTML tags and jQuery Mobile markup (e.g., data-role, data-theme, data-icon) to format an attractive touch interface for your app. Developing hybrid-based mobile apps is straightforward if you already know some basic standard Web development technology, such as HTML, CSS, JavaScript, and jQuery.

Modify the App's Controller (inline.js)

In the previous section, the initialization block in the view defers to the onSuccessSfdcMerchandise function of the controller to dynamically generate the HTML that renders Merchandise list items in the encompassing div, div_merchandise_list. In this step, you build the onSuccessSfdcMerchandise function.

Load the inline.js file and add the following controller action, which is somewhat similar to the sample functions.

```
// handle successful retrieval of Merchandise records
function onSuccessSfdcMerchandise(response) {
    // avoid jQuery conflicts
    var $j = jQuery.noConflict();

    // debug info to console
    SFHybridApp.logToConsole("onSuccessSfdcMerchandise: received " +
        response.totalSize + " merchandise records");

    // clear div_merchandise_list HTML
    $j("#div_merchandise_list").html("");

    // set the ul string var to a new UL
    var ul = $j('<ul data-role="listview" data-inset="true"
        data-theme="a" data-dividertheme="a"></ul>');

    // update div_merchandise_list with the UL
    $j("#div_merchandise_list").append(ul);

    // set the first li to display the number of records found
    // formatted using list-divider
    ul.append($j('<li data-role="list-divider">Merchandise records: '
```

```
                    + response.totalSize + '</li>'));

    // add an li for the merchandise being passed into the function
    // create array to store record information for click listener
    inventory = new Array();
    // loop through each record, using vars i and merchandise
    $j.each(response.records, function(i, merchandise) {
        // create an array element for each merchandise record
        inventory[merchandise.Id] = merchandise;
        // create a new li with the record's Name
        var newLi = $j("<li class='detailLink' data-id='" +
merchandise.Id
            + "'><a href='#'>" + merchandise.Name + "</a></li>");
        ul.append(newLi);
    });

    // render (create) the list of Merchandise records
    $j("#div_merchandise_list").trigger( "create" );
    // send the rendered HTML to the log for debugging
    SFHybridApp.logToConsole($j("#div_merchandise_list").html());

    // set up listeners for detailLink clicks
    $j(".detailLink").click(function() {
        // get the unique data-id of the record just clicked
        var id = $j(this).attr('data-id');
        //  using the id, get the record from the array created above

        var record = inventory[id];

        // use this info to set up various detail page information
        $j("#name").html(record.Name);
        $j("#quantity").val(record.Quantity__c);
        $j("#price").val(record.Price__c);
        $j("#detailpage").attr("data-id",record.Id);

        // change the view to the detailpage
        $j.mobile.changePage('#detailpage', {changeHash: true});

    });

}
```

The comments in the code explain each line. Notice the call to
`SFHybridApp.logToConsole()`; the JavaScript outputs rendered HTML to the console
log so that you can see what the code creates. Here's an excerpt of some sample output.

```
<ul data-role="listview" data-inset="true" data-theme="a"
    data-dividertheme="a" class="ui-listview ui-listview-inset
    ui-corner-all ui-shadow">
  <li data-role="list-divider" role="heading"
    class="ui-li ui-li-divider ui-btn ui-bar-a
ui-corner-top">Merchandise records: 6
  </li>
```

```
<li class="detailLink ui-btn ui-btn-up-a ui-btn-icon-right ui-li"
    data-id="a00E0000003BzSfIAK" data-theme="a">
  <div class="ui-btn-inner ui-li">
    <div class="ui-btn-text">
      <a href="#" class="ui-link-inherit">Tablet</a>
    </div>
  </div>
</li>
<li class="detailLink ui-btn ui-btn-up-a ui-btn-icon-right ui-li"
    data-id="a00E0000003BuUpIAK" data-theme="a">
  <div class="ui-btn-inner ui-li">
    <div class="ui-btn-text">
      <a href="#" class="ui-link-inherit">Laptop</a>
    </div>
  </div>
</li>

...

</ul>
```

In particular, notice how the code:

- creates a list of Merchandise records for display on the app's primary page
- creates each list item to display the Name of the Merchandise record
- creates each list item with unique link information that determines what the target detail page displays

Test the New App

Restart the simulator for your mobile app. When you do, the initial page should look similar to the following screen.

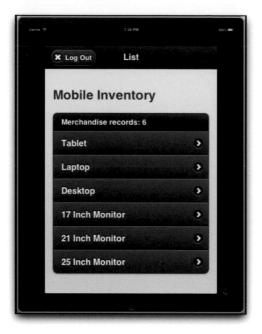

If you click any particular Merchandise record, nothing happens yet. The list functionality is useful, but even better when paired with the detail view. The next section helps you build the *detailpage* that displays when a user clicks a specific Merchandise record.

Create a Mobile Page for Detailed Information

In the previous topic, you modified the sample hybrid app so that, after it starts, it lists all Merchandise records and provides links to detail pages. In this topic, you finish the job by creating a *detailpage* view and updating the app's controller.

Create the App's detailpage View (index.html)

When a user clicks on a Merchandise record in the app's *mainpage* view, click listeners are in place to generate record-specific information and then load a view named *detailpage* that displays this information. To create the *detailpage* view, add the following div tag after the *mainpage* div tag.

```
<!-- Detail page, to display details when user clicks specific
Merchandise record -->
<div data-role="page" data-theme="b" id="detailpage">
    <!-- page header -->
    <div  data-role="header">
```

68

```
         <!-- button for going back to mainpage -->
         <a href='#mainpage' id="backInventory"
            class='ui-btn-left' data-icon='home'>
            Home
         </a>
         <!-- page title -->
         <h1>Edit</h1>
   </div>
   <!-- page content -->
   <div id="#content" data-role="content">
         <h2 id="name"></h2>
         <label for="price" class="ui-hidden-accessible">
            Price ($):</label>
         <input type="text" id="price" readonly="readonly"></input>
         <br/>
         <label for="quantity" class="ui-hidden-accessible">
            Quantity:</label>
         <!-- note that number is not universally supported -->
         <input type="number" id="quantity"></input>
         <br/>
         <a href="#" data-role="button" id="updateButton"
            data-theme="b">Update</a>
   </div>
</div>
```

The comments explain each part of the HTML. Basically, the view is a form that lets the user see a Merchandise record's Price and Quantity fields, and optionally update the record's Quantity.

Recall, the jQuery calls in the last part of the onSuccessSfdcMerchandise function (in inline.js) and updates the detail page elements with values from the target Merchandise record. Review that code, if necessary.

Modify the App's Controller (inline.js)

What happens when a user clicks the Update button in the new *detailpage* view? Nothing, yet. You need to modify the app's controller (inline.js) to handle clicks on that button.

In inline.js, add the following JavaScript to the tail end of the regLinkClickHandlers function.

```
// handle clicks to Update on detailpage
$j("#updateButton").click(function() {
    // update local information in the inventory array
    inventory[$j("#detailpage").attr("data-id")].Quantity__c =
$j("#quantity").val();
    currentRecord = inventory[$j("#detailpage").attr("data-id")];

    // strip out ID before updating the database
    var data = new Object();
    data.Quantity__c = currentRecord.Quantity__c;
    // update the database
```

```
        forcetkClient.update("Merchandise__c", currentRecord.Id,
            data,updateSuccess,onErrorSfdc);
});
```

The comments in the code explain each line. On success, the new handler calls the `updateSuccess` function, which is not currently in place. Add the following simple function to inline.js.

```
function updateSuccess(message) {
    alert("Item Updated");
}
```

Test the App

Restart the simulator for your mobile app. When you do, a detail page should appear when you click a specific Merchandise record and look similar to the following screen.

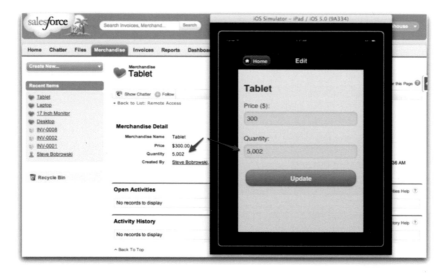

Feel free to update a record's quantity, and then check that you see the same quantity when you log into your DE org and view the record using the Force.com app UI (see above).

Support Social Collaboration with Chatter

From a developer's perspective, Chatter is a data model that includes several standard Force.com objects that manage social data for records in your org.

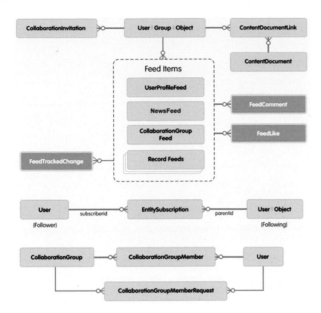

- **Feed Item**: Each feed item represents either a set of changes on a specific record or a post to a particular user or record. When a user posts to a feed, the ParentId of the resulting feed item holds the user's UserId. Some queries and statements, for example adding a comment, require the ID of a feed item.
- **FeedComment**: A FeedComment object stores comments and is a child object of an associated record feed item.

To access the Chatter data model, an app can use the Chatter REST API. The Chatter REST API provides access to Chatter feeds and social data such as feed items and comments via a standard JSON/XML-based API.

A full discussion of the Chatter REST API is beyond the scope of this topic. For a quick preview, see the *Chatter REST API Cheat Sheet*:
`http://wiki.developerforce.com/page/Cheat_Sheets`.

Modify the App's View (index.html)

To begin modifying your app, start by adding a new mobile page, `chatterpage`, to the app's view, in `index.html`. Go to https://gist.github.com/3644284 for the source code.

```
<!-- Detail page, to display Chatter Information -->
<div data-role="page" data-theme"b" id="chatterpage">
    <!-- page header -->
    <div data-role-"header">
```

```
        <!-- button for going back to detailpage -->
        <a href='#detailpage' id="backInventory" class='ui-btn-left'
data-icon='arrow-1'>
            Edit
        </a>
        <!-- page title -->
        <h1>Collaborate</h1>
    </div>
    <!-- page content -->
    <div id="#content" data-role="content">
        <h2 id="name"></h2>
        <div id="div_chatter_list">
            <!-- built dynamically by controller function
updateChatterList -->
        </div>
    </div>
</div>
```

Modify the App's Controller (inline.js)

The forcetk library, part of the Mobile SDK, is a wrapper around the Force.com REST API. However, at the time of this writing, it does not yet include suppport for the Chatter REST API. Therefore, the first modification necessary to your app's controller is to supplement the forcetk.Client object with three new functions. Prepend inline.js with the following snippet. Go to https://gist.github.com/3644304 for the source code.

```
// add select Chatter functions to forcetk
// get feed-items
forcetk.Client.prototype.chatterFeed = function(id, callback, error)
{
  this.ajax('/' + this.apiVersion + '/chatter/feeds/record/' + id +
'/feed-items', callback, error);
}

// post feed item
forcetk.Client.prototype.postChatterItem = function(id, text, callback,
 error) {
  this.ajax('/' + this.apiVersion + '/chatter/feeds/record/' + id +
'/feed-items', callback, error, "POST", '{ "body" : { "messageSegments"
 : [ { "type": "Text", "text" : "' + text + '" } ] } }');
}

// post feed comment
forcetk.Client.prototype.postChatterComment = function(id, text,
callback, error) {
  this.ajax('/' + this.apiVersion + '/chatter/feed-items/' + id +
'/comments', callback, error, "POST", '{ "body" : { "messageSegments"
 : [ { "type": "Text", "text" : "' + text + '" } ] } }');
}
```

Notice that these new functions call the Chatter REST API to get a feed's items (and all related posts and comments), post a new item to a feed, and post a new comment for an existing feed item.

Now append the following code to the `regLinkClickHandlers()` function to listen for clicks on a new button that you will soon add to the `detailpage`. Go to https://gist.github.com/3644348 for the source code.

```
// handle clicks to Collaborate on detailpage
$j("#chatterButton").click(function() {
  // using the id of the current Merchandise record, get its Chatter
feed items
  SFHybridApp.logToConsole("Getting Chatter");
  forcetkClient.chatterFeed($j("#detailpage").attr("data-id"),
updateChatterList, onErrorSfdc);
});
```

Notice that the new code above calls the new forcetkClient `chatterFeed() function` function. This call gets the feed items for the current Merchandise record, including related posts and comments with just one call to the database, making this function very efficient: an important design goal for mobile apps. This function call also yields to the `updateChatterList() function` function, which you need to add next along with a related `refreshChatterList function()`.

Add the following code to `inline.js` to add the two new functions. Go to https://gist.github.com/3644332 for the source code.

```
function refreshChatter(response) {
  forcetkClient.chatterFeed($j("#detailpage").attr("data-id"),
updateChatterList, onErrorSfdc);
}

function updateChatterList(response) {
  // output debug information to the log
  SFHybridApp.logToConsole("Got Chatter");
  SFHybridApp.logToConsole(response.items.length);

  // clear div_chatter_list HTML
  $j("#div_chatter_list").html("");

  // loop through all items and display UI
  $j.each(response.items, function(i, chatter) {
    // open a new div
    var newItemDiv = $j("<div class='ui-body ui-body-b'>");
    // append the item author name
    newItemDiv.append($j("<h5>" + chatter.actor.name + " said
...</h5>"));
    // append the item text
    newItemDiv.append($j("<p>" + chatter.body.text + "</p>"));

    // display item comments
```

```
    var newCommentDiv;
    $j.each(chatter.comments.comments, function(i, comment) {
      // reset newCommentDiv to open the div
      newCommentDiv = $j("<div class='ui-body ui-body-c'>");
      // append the item author name
     newCommentDiv.append($j("<h5>" + comment.user.name + " commented
...</h5>"));
      // append the item text
      newCommentDiv.append($j("<p>" + comment.body.text + "</p>"));
      // append the closing inner div tag
      newCommentDiv.append($j("</div>"));
      // append newCommentDiv to newItemDiv
      newItemDiv.append(newCommentDiv);
    });

    // append a comment button to the item
    newItemDiv.append($j("<a href='#' data-role='button' data-min='true'
 class='comment' data-theme='b' data-inline='true' data-icon='plus'
data-id='" + chatter.id + "'>Your Comment</a>"));

    // append the closing outer div tag
    newItemDiv.append($j("</div>"));

    // add the final item output to the div
    $j("#div_chatter_list").append(newItemDiv);

  });
  var newPostButtonDiv = $j("<a href='#' data-role='button'
data-min='true' class='post' data-theme='b' data-icon='plus'
data-inline='true' class='post'>New Post</a>")
  $j("#div_chatter_list").append(newPostButtonDiv);

  // set up listeners for chatterButton clicks
  $j("a.comment").click(function() {
    SFHybridApp.logToConsole("Commenting");

    var id = $j(this).attr('data-id');
    var post = prompt('Enter New Comment');
    if (post != null) {
      forcetkClient.postChatterComment(id, post, refreshChatter,
onErrorSfdc);
    }

  });

  // set up listeners for chatterButton clicks
  $j("a.post").click(function() {
    SFHybridApp.logToConsole("Posting");

    var id = $j("#detailpage").attr("data-id");
    SFHybridApp.logToConsole('detailpage id.');
    SFHybridApp.logToConsole(id);
    var post = prompt('Enter New Post');
    if (post != null) {
      forcetkClient.postChatterItem(id, post, refreshChatter,
onErrorSfdc);
```

```
  }
});

// render the final chatter list
$j("#div_chatter_list").trigger("create");
// log debug information
SFHybridApp.logToConsole('Item output div.');
SFHybridApp.logToConsole($j("#div_chatter_list").html());

// change the view to the detailpage, tracking the location change
$j.mobile.changePage('#chatterpage', {
  changeHash: true
});
}
```

Try Out the App

Now that the app's view and controller have been updated to support Chatter, try out the app and test it out. Rebuild the app, and run it in your IDE's simulator. Then click into a Merchandise record that you know has some Chatter feed items associated with it (use the Warehouse app in your browser if you need to find such a record). On the detailpage of the mobile app, tap the new **Collaborate** button.

Tapping **Collaborate** takes you to the new chatterpage view of the mobile app, which displays all the Chatter feed items, including related posts and comments. Feel free to add both a new post or comment on an existing post and see that your work is reflected in the Warehouse app.

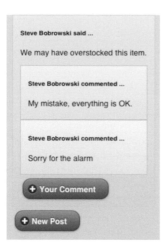

You've successfully made your mobile app social such that users can collaborate on Merchandise records!

iOS Hybrid Sample Application

The sample applications contained under the hybrid/ folder are designed around the PhoneGap SDK. Before you can work with those applications, you need to download and install the PhoneGap SDK, which you can get from the PhoneGap website. You can find more detailed installation instructions, as well as documentation for working with the PhoneGap SDK, in the Getting Started Guide.

The hybrid sample applications are configured to look for the PhoneGap iOS Framework in `/Users/Shared/PhoneGap/Frameworks/PhoneGap.framework`, and might not load the framework properly if it is located elsewhere. To find out if the PhoneGap framework is properly linked in the sample project, take the following action:

1. Open the project in XCode.
2. In Project Navigator, expand the Frameworks folder.
3. If PhoneGap.framework is listed among the configured frameworks, your project should be fine, and no further action is necessary.

If you do not see the PhoneGap framework, or otherwise get compilation errors related to the PhoneGap Framework not being found (e.g. Undefined symbols for architecture i386: "_OBJC_METACLASS_$_PhoneGapDelegate"), you will need to add the PhoneGap Framework to the sample project:

1. Open the Xcode project of the sample application.
2. In the Project Navigator, right-click or control-click the Frameworks folder, and select **Add files to "Project Name..."**.
3. Navigate to the `PhoneGap.framework` folder (the default location is `/Users/Shared/PhoneGap/Frameworks/PhoneGap.framework/`), and click **Add**.

The sample application project should now build and run cleanly.

Android Hybrid Sample Application

Inside the `HYBRID_DIR`, you will find several projects:

- **SampleApps/ContactExplorer**: The `ContactExplorer` sample app uses PhoneGap (aka "callback") to retrieve local device contacts. It also uses the `forcetk.js` toolkit to implement REST transactions with the Salesforce REST API. The app uses the OAuth2 support in Salesforce SDK to obtain OAuth credentials, then propagates those credentials to `forcetk.js` by sending a javascript event.
- **SampleApps/VFConnector**: The VFConnector sample app demonstrates how to wrap a Visualforce page in a native container. This example assumes that your org has a Visualforce page called `BasicVFTest`. The app first obtains OAuth login credentials using the Salesforce SDK OAuth2 support, then uses those credentials to set appropriate webview cookies for accessing Visualforce pages.
- **SmartStorePluginTest**: Tests for the SmartStore phonegap plugin.

The sample applications contained under the hybrid/ folder are designed around the PhoneGap SDK. Before you can work with those applications, you need to download and install the `1.0.0` (or later) version of the PhoneGap SDK, which you can get from the PhoneGap website. You can find more detailed installation instructions, as well as documentation for working with the PhoneGap SDK, in the Getting Started Guide.

The hybrid sample applications are configured to look for the PhoneGap Android Framework in /Users/Shared/PhoneGap/Frameworks/PhoneGap.framework, and might not load the framework properly if it is located elsewhere. To find out if the PhoneGap framework is properly linked in the sample project, take the following action:

1. Open the project in Eclipse.
2. In Project Navigator, expand the project folder.
3. If PhoneGap.framework is listed among the configured frameworks, your project should be fine, and no further action is necessary.

If you do not see the PhoneGap framework, or otherwise get compilation errors related to the PhoneGap Framework not being found (for example, 'Undefined symbols for architecture i386: "_OBJC_METACLASS_$_PhoneGapDelegate"'), you will need to add the PhoneGap Framework to the sample project.

1. Open the project of the sample application.
2. In the Project Navigator, right-click or control-click the Frameworks folder, and select **Add files to "Project Name..."**.
3. Navigate to the PhoneGap.framework folder (the default location is /Users/Shared/PhoneGap/Frameworks/PhoneGap.framework/), and click **Add**.

The sample application project should now build and run cleanly.

Ho Ho Ho

Chapter 7

Hybrid Development with Mobile Components for Visualforce

The flexible component infrastructure of Visualforce makes it possible to wrap low-level code into reusable components for developing custom apps on the Force.com platform. You can leverage Visualforce to create hybrid mobile applications.

The open-source Mobile Components for Visualforce library contains lightweight UI components that generate cross-platform HTML5 output. These apps can be deployed in the browser or embedded inside the hybrid Mobile SDK container. The source code for this library is available on Github:
`https://github.com/forcedotcom/MobileComponents/tree/master/Visualforce`

The component library enables any Visualforce developer to quickly and easily build mobile applications without having to dig deep into complex mobile frameworks and design patterns. This library includes the frameworks and best practices of mobile development that can be used with simple component interfaces.

Mobile Components for VisualforceArchitecture

The following image gives you a quick overview of the architecture of Mobile Components for Visualforce.

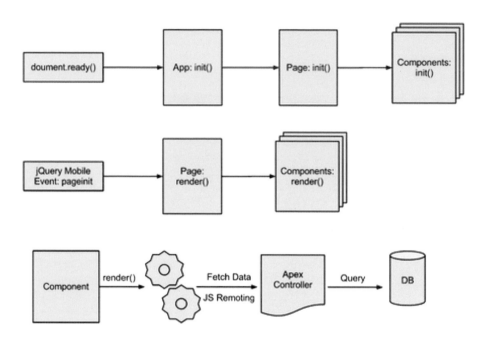

Visualforce Mobile Open Components

The Visualforce library consists of the following components:

- **App Component** — This component provides all the settings and architecture pieces (including jQuery and jQuery Mobile) for mobile app development.
- **Navigation Component** — Navigation Component can be used to create hooks for navigation between various jQuery Mobile pages.
- **SplitView Template** — This template provides the split view components on the page. In landscape mode, it provides a left menu section and a broad main section. In portrait mode, it turns the left menu into a popover.
- **List Component** — List Component provides a quick and easy way to render a record list for any sObject. One can easily manage the behavior of the component by using the various attributes or the JavaScript hooks, on this component.

- **Detail Component** — Detail Component provides a quick and easy way to render the details for any sObject. One can easily manage the behavior by using the various attributes or the JavaScript hooks.
- **Page Component** — Page Component provides a jQuery Mobile wrapper with `data-role="page"`.
- **Header Component** — Header Component provides a jQuery Mobile wrapper with `data-role="header"` for header sections inside a Page component.
- **Content Component** — Content Component provides a jQuery Mobile wrapper with `data-role="content"` for content sections inside a Page component.
- **Footer Component** — Footer Component provides a jQuery Mobile wrapper with `data-role="footer"` for footer sections inside a Page component.

 Note: These Visualforce components are open-source and are not officially supported by Salesforce.

Visualforce App Component

All mobile Visualforce pages built using this component library need to be wrapped inside the App component. The App component provides the primary architectural pieces, such as viewport settings, javascripts, stylesheets etc., for the mobile app. The `debug` attribute on App components lets you specify if you are running in development or production mode, and delivers the minified version of assets for the latter case.

```
<c:App debug="true"></c:App>
```

Visualforce Navigation Component

The navigation component provides a way to create hooks for navigation between various jQuery Mobile pages.

Visualforce SplitView Template

The SplitViewTemplate is used inside the App component. The split view page provides a slim left section for list view, and a wider right section to show the record details.

```
<apex:composition template="SplitViewTemplate"></apex:composition>
```

SplitViewTemplate consists of two sections you need to define.

- "menu" is the left section of the split view in landscape mode. This section becomes a popover when a user rotates the tablet to switch to the portrait mode.
- "main" is the right wide section of the split view. This section is always visible on the tablet in both portrait and landscape modes.

```
<apex:define name="menu">
    <c:Page name="list">
        <c:Header >
          <h1 style="font-size: 20px; margin: 0px;">All Contacts</h1>

        </c:Header>
        <c:Content >
            <c:List sobject="Contact" labelField="Name"
subLabelField="Account.Name" sortByField="FirstName" listFilter="true"/>

        </c:Content>
    </c:Page>
 </apex:define>
```

Visualforce Page Component

The Page component provides an important wrapper to define the fixed header and footer components with a scrollable content section in between.

- The Header component is used to define the fixed title of the section.
- The Content component describes the scrollable content section.
- Within the body of Content component, the List component is used to fetch and display the contact list.

Visualforce Header Component

Provides a jQuery Mobile wrapper with data-role="header" for header sections inside a Page component. Header components often include a <H1> tag. The header and footer components are fixed, and scrollable content can go between them.

Visualforce Content Component

The Content component describes the scrollable content section, including the List and Detail components.

Within the Content component, the List and Detail components respect the Object, Field, and Record visibility settings so you can develop the applications using these components without worrying about data security. Also, one can easily override the CSS styles of these components to give it a look and feel as required by your project. If you have used jQuery mobile, you can easily see that the page, header, footer, and content components actually use the jQuery mobile properties to enable the mobile user experience. So, while using this component library, you can easily leverage other features of jQuery mobile too.

Visualforce List Component

The List component is used to fetch and display records. The sObject attribute on List component is used to specify the sObject type for which the list view needs to be created. Other attributes, such as labelField, subLabelField, sortByField, and listFilter, are used to specify the behavior and display properties of this list.

```
<c:List sobject="Contact" labelField="Name" subLabelField="Account.Name"
 sortByField="FirstName" listFilter="true"/>
```

Visualforce Detail Component

The Detail component takes the sObject type as an attribute and generates the mobile layout with details of the associated record. The mobile layout of the record is driven by the Page layout associated to the current user profile and associated record type. This gives the administrator the flexibility to update the mobile layout by using the standard Salesforce page layout manager without further code modifications.

```
<apex:define name="main">
    <c:Page name="main">
        <c:Header >
            <h1 style="font-size: 22px; margin: 0px;">Contact
Details</h1>
        </c:Header>
        <c:Content >
            <c:Detail sobject="Contact"/>
        </c:Content>
    </c:Page>
</apex:define>
```

Visualforce Footer Component

Provides a jQuery Mobile wrapper with `data-role="footer"` for header sections inside a Page component. The header and footer components are fixed, and scrollable content can go between them.

Installing the Components

Before you can start using the components you need to Install the package of components and enable the remote access points.

1. Grab the source code from git

```
git clone https://github.com/forcedotcom/MobileComponents.git
```

Next you'll need to deploy the Force.com metadata found in the `MobileComponents/Visualforce/src` folder to your destination org with Force.com Workbench using following steps:

1. Create a ZIP archive of `MobileComponents/Visualforce/src`.
2. Navigate to the Workbench: `https://workbench.developerforce.com/`.
3. Log in using your salesforce.com credentials and confirm that Workbench may access your data.
4. Click **Migration > Deploy**.
5. Click **Choose File** (or **Browse**, depending on your browser), and select the ZIP archive file created above.
6. Enable **Rollback on Error**.
7. Click **Next** and then **Deploy**.

Finally you need to configure a remote access point in your Salesforce org,

1. Log into your org and cick **Setup > Administration Setup > Security Controls > Remote Site Settings**.
2. Click **New Remote Site**, then create a new site by specifying your org's instance URL for the Remote Site URL. For example, if your org is on instance NA1, the Remote Site URL will be `https://na1.salesforce.com`.

You should now be all set and ready to use Mobile Components for Visualforce. To see the sample Contact viewer app in action, navigate to the following page: `https://<remote site url>/apex/MobilePage`

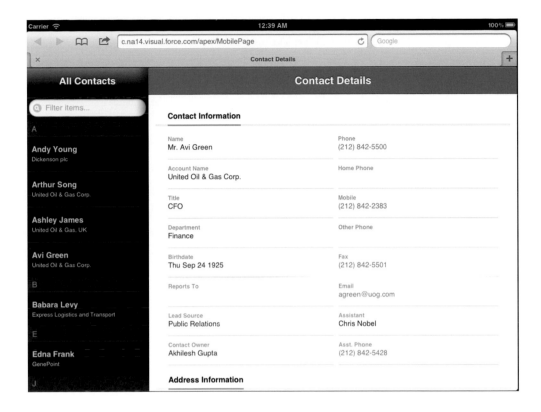

Creating Your First Tablet Page

Mobile Components for Visualforce includes a couple of sample Visualforce pages (MobilePage and MobilePageWithComponents) that demonstrate how to use the components for a tablet application.

Now take a look at the MobilePage and see how it is built for a tablet to display the list of Contacts and related details. All mobile Visualforce pages built using Mobile Components for Visualforce need to be wrapped inside the App component. The App component provides the primary architectural pieces, such as viewport settings, JavaScripts, style sheets, etc., for the mobile app. The debug attribute of an App component let's you specify whether the app is running in development or production mode and whether to deliver the minified version of assets for the later case.

```
<c:App debug="true"></c:App>
```

Inside the `App` component, you can specify the body of the mobile app. In this case, you build a split view page, which provides a slim left section for list view, and a wider right section to show the record details. To do this, you compose the page by using the `SplitViewTemplate` which is part of this component library.

```
<apex:composition template="SplitViewTemplate"></apex:composition>
```

`SplitViewTemplate` consists of two sections that you need to define.

- menu — The left section of the split view in landscape mode. This section becomes a popover when user rotates the tablet to switch to the portrait mode.
- main — The right, wide section of the split view. This section is always visible on the tablet in both portrait and landscape modes.

Now define the content inside these sections of the split view. Here's how to define the content for the left menu section:

```
<apex:define name="menu">
    <c:Page name="list">
        <c:Header>
            <h1 style="font-size: 20px; margin: 0px;">All Contacts</h1>

        </c:Header>
        <c:Content>
            <c:List sobject="Contact" labelField="Name"
              subLabelField="Account.Name" sortByField="FirstName"
              listFilter="true"/>
        </c:Content>
    </c:Page>
</apex:define>
```

While defining the content of the left menu section, you use the `Page` component, which provides an important wrapper to define the fixed header and footer components with a scrollable content section in between. Within the `Page` component, you use the `Header` component to define the fixed title of the section. Following the header, you use the `Content` component to describe the scrollable content section. Within the body of `Content` component, you use the `List` component to fetch and display the Contact list. Use the `sObject` attribute on the `List` component to specify the `sObject` type for creating the list view. Use other attributes such as `labelField`, `subLabelField`, `sortByField`, and `listFilter` to specify the behavior and display properties of this list (hopefully, the attribute names are self-explanatory).

```
<c:List sobject="Contact" labelField="Name" subLabelField="Account.Name"

    sortByField="FirstName"listFilter="true"/>
```

Now take a look at the content inside the `main` section of the split view.

```
<c:Page name="main">
    <c:Header >
        <h1 style="font-size: 22px; margin: 0px;">Contact Details</h1>

        </c:Header>
        <c:Content >
            <c:Detail sobject="Contact"/>
        </c:Content>
    </c:Page>
</apex:define>
```

Similar to `menu` section, you use the `Page` component to define the contents of `main` section and to enable the use of `Header`, `Footer`, and `Content` components. Using the `Header` component, you specify the title to this section. Following the `Header` component, use the `Content` component to specify the `Detail` component. The `Detail` component takes the sObject type as an attribute and generates the mobile layout with details of the associated record. The `Page` layout associated to the current user profile and associated record type drives the mobile layout of the record. This gives administrators the flexibility to update the mobile layout by using the standard Salesforce `Page` layout manager and avoids a requirement for code modifications.

```
<c:Detail sobject="Contact"/>
```

Easy Integration

The `List` and `Detail` components respect your org's `Object`, `Field`, and `Record` visibility settings. Consequently, you can develop apps using these components without having to modify existing security settings. Also, you can easily override the CSS styles of these components to give them a look and feel as required by your project.

If you already know jQuery Mobile, notice that the `Page`, `Header`, `Footer`, and `Content` components actually use the jQuery Mobile properties to enable the mobile user experience. So, while using this component library, you can easily leverage other features of jQuery Mobile too.

Creating a Mobile Component for Visualforce

You can look at generic web pages on any smartphone or tablet, but the experience is quite a bit better when the UI is optimized for mobile. If you're a Visualforce developer, you're already half-way down the path to mobile-optimized applications. The HTML5 movement is in full swing, and there are a number of mobile-optimized web frameworks that make it easy to leverage its features. Already in this chapter you've seen how Visualforce Mobile Open Components leverage jQuery Mobile and make it easy to generate mobile apps that use Salesforce data. But you can also create those components yourself.

Introducing jQuery Mobile Pages

Take a look at a **jQuery Mobile** page from a high level. The framework heavily relies on tagging elements with the *data-role* attribute for block-level page layouts, specifying one of a variety of values. On page load, the jQuery Mobile framework searches the document for these elements and takes control of them, adding behavior and styles that brands it as a mobile app. For example, an element with a *data-role* value of *page* defines it as the most basic building block of a jQuery Mobile application -- a single mobile-optimized page. When the page is parsed, jQuery Mobile fills the screen with its contents, treating it as a single page in the mobile app.

```
<!-- Ex. jQuery Mobile Page -->
<div data-role="page">
  <h1>My Page</h1>
</div><!-- /page -->
```

There are other **data-role attributes**, which are designed to be used together to create a mobile app. A *page* section looks best when it has a *header* section on top, a *content* section in the middle, and a *footer* section on the bottom. When elements with these *data-role* values are nested inside a *page*, the framework ensures that it looks as it should and that it looks consistent across devices. Besides nesting elements, you can combine app sections horizontally as well. If a *page* section has **sibling *page* sections**, jQuery Mobile displays only the first page section when loading the app, and removes the others from the DOM to keep it lean and responsive. Don't worry, those pages are cached, and can be displayed by hash-linking to them by page ID, complete with page load and transition animations.

```
<!-- Ex. jQuery Mobile Page 2 -->
<div data-role="page2">
  <div data-role="header">
    <h1>My Title</h1>
  </div><!-- /header -->

  <div data-role="content">
    <p>Hello world</p>
  </div><!-- /content -->
</div><!-- /page -->
```

Understanding Visualforce Mobile Components

jQuery Mobile has list views, navigation, and a variety of form inputs, which is perfect for displaying and entering data on a mobile device. Combine this with a data source, such as your Salesforce org, and you can quickly create mobile apps filled with meaningful and useful data. With this in mind, let's take a look at the Mobile Components for Visualforce library. Mobile Components for Visualforce is an open source library that lets Visualforce developers easily use a mobile app framework, like jQuery Mobile, by providing easy-to-use components. At the time of this writing, the library is relatively new and doesn't support every type of mobile view and widget, but it has a strong core that makes creating new components to fill these gaps pretty easy.

The following figure illustrates the Mobile Components for Visualforce architecture.

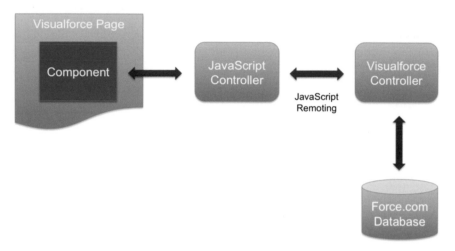

A Visualforce page contains a variety of components, including mobile components provided by Mobile Components for Visualforce. A mobile component relies on a JavaScript controller, a JavaScript Remoting bridge, and a Visualforce controller to interact with the Force.com database.

Building Custom Mobile Components for Visualforce

Now that you understand the architecture of Mobile Components for Visualforce, let's make a new component so that you can see exactly how it's done. When it was first open-sourced, the Mobile Components for Visualforce project consisted of only a handful of components, including a List, a Navigation, and a Detail component. However, the jQuery Mobile framework supports many other components, which means there is much room for growth in this project.

The following figure on the left shows an example of the *List* component that is already part of Mobile Components for Visualforce. But wouldn't it be cool to show a list of your org's users, complete with their profile pictures, such as in the following figure on the right?

jQuery Mobile has this type of list, called a **Thumbnails List**, which gives us a good head-start. In this section, we're going to walk through the code that builds such a component, both high-level in justifying the responsibility of each code snippet and low-level by showing and explaining implementation details. With such an approach, this section is intended to be useful as an introduction and reference for readers who may wish to create other types of components.

Following Along

If you would like to have a working example to follow along:

1. Create a new, free **Developer Edition (DE) org.**
2. Install the **example managed package** to build everything related to a new *ThumbnailsList* component.

This package includes:

- A custom fork of the Mobile Components for Visualforce framework that includes some modified versions of provided components, such as Page.
- The *ThumbnailList* component with a demo page named *ThumbnailList*.

Reviewing the Custom Visualforce Mobile Component

The following code is the custom *ThumbnailList* component. If you installed the sample package in a DE org, you can find this code by clicking > **Setup** > **Develop** > **Components** > **ThumbnailList**.

```
<apex:component controller="ThumbnailListController">
  <!-- Content -->
  <apex:attribute name="sObjectType" type="String" required="true"
assignTo="{!config.sObjectType}" description=""/>
  <apex:attribute name="filter" type="String" required="false"
assignTo="{!config.filter}" description="owner|recent|follower"/>
```

```
  <apex:attribute name="filterClause" type="String" required="false"
assignTo="{!config.filterClause}"
description="SOQL WHERE clause to use to filter list records."/>
  <!-- UI -->
  <apex:attribute name="imageUrlField" type="String" required="true"
assignTo="{!config.imageUrlField}" description=""/>
  <apex:attribute name="labelField" type="String" required="true"
assignTo="{!config.labelField}" description=""/>
  <apex:attribute name="subLabelField" type="String" required="true"
assignTo="{!config.subLabelField}" description=""/>
  <apex:attribute name="listItemStyleClass" type="String"
assignTo="{!config.listItemStyleClass}" description=""/>
  <apex:attribute name="sortByField" type="String" required="true"
assignTo="{!config.sortByField}" description=""/>
  <apex:attribute name="listDividerStyleClass" type="String"
assignTo="{!config.listDividerStyleClass}" description=""/>
  <apex:attribute name="listDividerStyleClass" type="String"
assignTo="{!config.listDividerStyleClass}" description=""/>
  <apex:attribute name="listFilter" type="Boolean" default="false"
description=""/>
  <!-- Behaviour -->
  <apex:attribute name="nextPage" type="String"
assignTo="{!config.nextPage}" description=""/>
  <apex:attribute name="jsCtlrName" type="String"
assignTo="{!config.jsCtlrName}" default="$V.ThumbnailListController"
description="Custom JavaScript handler to manage client-side lifecycle
 and behavior."/>
  <apex:attribute name="debug" type="Boolean" assignTo="{!config.debug}"
 default="false" description=""/>

  <!-- VF/HTML -->
  <apex:includeScript value="{!URLFOR($Resource[ThumbnailListJS])}"/>

  <apex:includeScript value="{!URLFOR($Resource.ICanHaz)}"/>

  <apex:outputPanel layout="inline" id="list">
     <ul data-role="listview" data-filter="{!listFilter}"></ul>
  </apex:outputPanel>

  <script>$V.App.registerComponent('{!$Component.list}',
{!configAsJson});</script>
</apex:component>
```

- Line 1: Notice that the component uses a custom Visualforce controller ThumbnailListController. We'll examine this controller soon.
- Lines 3-20: These are run-time parameters that the component accepts. When a Visualforce page utilizes this component, the component passes the associated attribute values to its controller, which in turn passes them on to its JavaScript controller to reference. Note that the *assignTo* parameters of each attribute reference the *config* object, which is defined on the Visualforce controller. We'll review both of these controllers in subsequent sections.
- Line 23: This line includes the custom JavaScript controller, which is stored in the database as a static resource. We'll review this controller soon.

- Line 24: The example Visualforce page in the next section includes a list item template that uses **Mustache** tags, which is a well-known logic-less template tool. Therefore, we'll need a JavaScript library that can parse the tags and fill the template with data. The Mustache-supporting template tool that we are using for this component is called **ICanHaz**, which is freely available as open source code. This line includes ICanHaz, which is also stored in our database as a static resource.
- Lines 26-28: A standard `outputPanel` to which the list items we generate will be appended.
- Line 30: All components must register with the framework before they can render on page requests, which is what this line is doing. For future discussions, note that this is where the JavaScript controller receives the *config* object that is stored in the Visualforce controller. This *config* object is used by both Visualforce and JavaScript controllers, as it communicates essential information between them, such as the Visualforce controller's name, the root element of the list, and whether the mobile app is in debug mode and permits debug messages. This function parameter is expecting a JSON string, so there's a method in the Visualforce controller, *getConfigAsJson*, that serializes the *config* object into JSON.

Reviewing an Example Visualforce Page

Now let's review the sample Visualforce page that uses the new ThumbnailList component. If you installed the sample package in a DE org, you can find this code by clicking **Setup** > **Develop** > **Pages** > **ThumbnailList**.

```
<!-- ThumbnailList.page -->
<apex:page showHeader="false"  standardStylesheets="false" cache="false"
 doctype="html-5.0">
    <!-- Templates -->
    <script id="rowItemTempl" type="text/html">
      {{#records}}
      <li data-corners="false"
          data-shadow="false"
          data-iconshadow="true"
          data-wrapperels="div"
          data-icon="arrow-r"
          data-iconpos="right"
          data-theme="c"
          data-item-context="{{Id}}"
          class="ui-btn ui-btn-icon-right ui-li-has-arrow ui-li
ui-li-has-thumb ui-btn-up-c">

        <div class="ui-btn-inner ui-li">
          <div class="ui-btn-text">
          <a href="/ThumbnailList#userDetail" class="ui-link-inherit">

            <img src="{{FullPhotoUrl}}" class="ui-li-thumb">
            <h3 class="ui-li-heading">{{Name}}</h3>
            <p class="ui-li-desc">{{Phone}}</p>
          </a>
          </div>
          <span class="ui-icon ui-icon-arrow-r ui-icon-shadow"> </span>
```

```
        </div>
      </li>
      {{/records}}
    </script>
<!-- Declare a new app, with one page. -->
<c:App debug="true">
    <c:Page name="list"
            theme="touch"
            debug="true">
        <c:Header >
            <h1 style="font-size: 20px; margin: 0px;">All Users</h1>
        </c:Header>
        <c:Content >
            <c:ThumbnailList sObjectType="User"
                    imageUrlField="FullPhotoUrl"
                    labelField="Name"
                    subLabelField="Phone"
                    sortByField="Name"
                    listFilter="true"
                    filter="recent"
                    debug="true"/>
        </c:Content>
    </c:Page>
</c:App>
<style>
    [data-role="panel"][data-id="main"] [data-role="page"].ui-page
.ui-content {
        background: white;
    }
    .ui-body-touch, .ui-overlay-touch {
        font-family: Helvetica, Arial, sans-serif
    }
</style>
</apex:page>
```

First, let's discuss the HTML template defined by the *<script id="rowItemTempl">* tag, Lines 3-28. This template is an extension of the HTML for the **example Thumbnail List** on the jQuery Mobile site. At the beginning of this article, we described how jQuery Mobile reads elements that have specific properties. We need to use this array of properties on the *li* tags to ensure they are styled properly by jQuery Mobile when they are added to the page's DOM.

Also, notice that the *rowItemTempl* template uses **Mustache** tags - ({{records}}, {{Id}}, {{FullPhotoURL}}, and {{Phone}}) - as placeholders for field values to simplify the process of transforming JSON data into HTML elements. After parsing this template with ICanHaz (discussed previously), we can push JSON data into it, which we receive from our JavaScript Remoting requests to the Visualforce controller. This quickly and easily creates a list of *li* tags, each with data specific to each record retrieved, and each with particular attributes that jQuery Mobile can parse and handle. With this complete, we now have a complete way of getting Salesforce data and rendering it to the page such that it looks like a native mobile app.

In the body of the page, review Lines 38-45. All that's necessary is a reference to the custom *ThumbnailList* component (discussed previously), providing values for each of the component's attributes.

Reviewing the JavaScript Controller

Next, let's review the JavaScript controller. Remember, one of the main functions of the JavaScript controller is to serve as a data bridge to the component's Visualforce controller, which we'll discuss in the next section. If you installed the sample package in a DE org, you can find this code by clicking **Setup** > **Develop** > **Site Resources** > **ThumbnailListJS** > **View File**.

```
(function($) {
  $V.ThumbnailListController = $V.Component.extend({
  init: function(config) {
    this._super(config);
  },
  prepare: function() {
    this._super();
  },
  render: function() {
    this._super();
    // Load records from the server, and give it a function to handle
 the response.
    $.mobile.showPageLoadingMsg();
    var serverRecords = this.requestRecords(this.requestRecordsHandler);

    $.mobile.hidePageLoadingMsg();
  },
  requestRecords: function(responseHandler) {
    // Specify any parameter values for the component's Visualforce
controller.
    var configProxy = {
      sObjectType: this.config.sObjectType,
      imageUrlField: this.config.imageUrlField,
      labelField: this.config.labelField,
      subLabelField: this.config.subLabelField,
      sortByField: this.config.sortByField
    };
    $V.App.getFn(this.config.serverCtlrName).getRecordsForConfig(
      this.config,
      // Callback
      (function(that, fn) {
        return function(result, event) {
          fn.apply(that, arguments);
        };
      })(this, responseHandler)
    );
  },
  requestRecordsHandler: function(result, event) {
    // See what the response looks like.
    $V.App.log.debug(this.config.serverCtlrName + '.getRecords response:
', result);
```

```
      // Transform the response list of records to match the template.
      var model = {};
      model.records = [];
      for (var i = 0; i < result.length; i++) {
        var record = result[i];
        model.records.push(record);
      }
      $V.App.log.debug('Finished model: ', model);
      // Push the data into the template. This templating engine is
called
      // ICanHaz, which is a wrapper around Mustache templating.
      // This command looks for a template stored as HTML inside
      // <script id="rowItemTempl" type="text/html"><script> tags.
      var listItemsMarkup = ich.rowItemTempl(model, true);
      $V.App.log.debug('Template result: ', listItemsMarkup);
      // Render the markup to the DOM.
      $ul = this.$me.find('ul');
      $ul.html(listItemsMarkup);
      // After mark up is rendered, do other stuff, like create handlers
  for tap events.
      //this.applyEvents($ul);
    }
  });
}) (jQuery);
```

Line 2 demonstrates the syntax to use when inheriting the framework's *$V.Component* class. How to implement this JavaScript controller, even though it is noted in the documentation, needs more clarification. When extending this framework class, we need to fulfill the implied contract, which is to implement the *init*, *prepare*, and *render* methods, and call the *this._super()* method before any of their implementation logic. You can see this in Lines 3-25.

Let's look deeper at the significance of these methods. Why are they necessary, and how should they be implemented? These methods are called from the framework, and the framework expects them to perform specific actions. The framework will call a component's *init* method when the object is first created, the *prepare* method right before rendering the component, and the *render* method when the user requests the component to be rendered. With a simple implementation like ours, we don't need to do anything to setup this object, so we can leave the *init* method empty. For the same reason, we can also leave the *prepare* method empty. Our efforts are focused on the *render* method, in which we generate the list items by using the HTML template in our page (see previous section). This render method:

- Fetches records from the server by calling the JavaScript Remoting method in our Visualforce controller, *getRecordsForConfig*. We'll take a look at this method in the next section.
- Handles the server response with the *requestRecordsHandler* method, which translates the record data into HTML strings, using the *rowItemTempl* template, and appends it to the *ul* element in the DOM.

Reviewing the Visualforce Controller

Finally, let's explore what's happening in the Visualforce controller that supports the new *ThumbnailList* component. If you installed the sample package in a DE org, you can find this code by clicking **Setup** > **Develop** > **Apex Classes** > **ThumbnailList**.

```apex
public class ThumbnailListController {

    public ThumbnailListConfig config {get; set;}

    // Parameter object to pass between JavaScript and Visualforce
controllers.
    public virtual class ThumbnailListConfig {
        public Boolean debug { get; set; }
        // The elemId is generated in VF and sent to client.
        public String elemId {get; set;}
        public String sObjectType {get; set;}
        public String imageUrlField {get; set;}
        public String labelField {get; set;}
        public String subLabelField {get; set;}
        public String sortByField {get; set;}
        public String filter { get; set; }
        public String filterClause {get; set;}
        public String listItemStyleClass { get; set; }
        public String listDividerStyleClass { get; set; }
        public String nextPage { get; set; }
        public String serverCtlrName = 'ThumbnailListController';
        public String jsCtlrName {get; set;}
    }

    // constructor
    public ThumbnailListController() {
        this.config = new ThumbnailListConfig();
    }

    private final static String THUMBNAIL_LIST_JS = 'ThumbnailListJS';

    public String getThumbnailListJS() {
        return config.debug ? THUMBNAIL_LIST_JS : (THUMBNAIL_LIST_JS
+ 'Min');
    }

    @RemoteAction
    public static List<Sobject> getRecordsForConfig(ThumbnailListConfig
config) {
        System.debug('--- config: ' + config);
        Set<String> fieldsToQuerySet = new Set<String>();
        fieldsToQuerySet.add(config.imageUrlField);
        fieldsToQuerySet.add(config.labelField);
        fieldsToQuerySet.add(config.subLabelField);
        fieldsToQuerySet.add(config.sortByField);

        List<Sobject> recordList = ThumbnailListController.getRecords(

                config.sObjectType,
```

```
                    fieldsToQuerySet,
                    UserInfo.getUserId()
                    );

        return recordList;
    }
    public static List<Sobject> getRecords(
            String sObjectType,
            Set<String> fieldsToQuerySet,
            Id userId) {

        List<Sobject> recordList = new List<Sobject>();
        String queryString = ' ';

        // Build the Select clause.
        queryString += 'SELECT ';
        for (String field : fieldsToQuerySet)
            queryString += (field + ',');
    queryString = queryString.subString(0, queryString.length()-1);


        // Build the From clause.
        queryString += ' FROM ' + sObjectType;

        // Build the Where clause.
        queryString += ' WHERE ';
        queryString += ' LastModifiedById = \'' + userId + '\'';

        recordList = Database.query(queryString);
        return recordList;
    }

    public virtual String getConfigAsJson() {
        String configStr = JSON.serialize(this.config);
        System.debug(configStr);
        return configStr;
    }
}
}
```

- Lines 3-27: These methods set up the *config* object. Remember, both the JavaScript controller and Visualforce controller, discussed earlier, rely on the *config* object to communicate essential information back and forth.
- Lines 76-80: A method to serialize the *config* object as JSON, meant to be passed to the *$V.App.registerComponent* method, in Line 30 of the component.
- Lines 29-32: A script include tag in the *ThumbnailList* component itself (Line 23) relies on this *getThumbnailListJS* method to get the name of the JavaScript controller's file name. By allowing a method to supply the name of this file, we can inject logic that returns either the full source code version or a minified version. A minified version would be more suitable when deploying this code to production, since it is a smaller filesize and a user can load the script faster.
- Lines 34-50: The *getRecordsForConfig* method is the JavaScript Remoting method that links together the JavaScript and Visualforce controllers. When called by the JavaScript

controller's *requestRecords* function, *getRecordsForConfig* does some setup and calls the*getRecords* method in the Visualforce controller to fetch and return the requested records.

- Lines 51-74: The *getRecords* method in the Visualforce controller fetches and returns the requested records.

Wrapping Up

You can see the fruits of your labor and open the example page that uses the component you just looked at. In your DE org, navigate to*<pod>.salesforce.com/apex/ThumbnailList* to see the demo page that uses the new component. These components will help bring mobile app development to a wider audience, enabling the thousands of Visualforce developers out there to easily create mobile apps.

Chapter 8

HTML5 Development

HTML5 lets you create lightweight interfaces without installing software on the mobile device; any mobile, touch or desktop device can access the same interface. You can create an HTML5 application that uses Visualforce to deliver the HTML content and fetches record data from Force.com using JavaScript remoting for Apex controllers. The sample application also utilizes the jQuery Mobile library for the user interface.

HTML5 Development Requirements

- You must create a remote access application. See Creating a Remote Access Application.
- Some knowledge of Apex and Visualforce is necessary.
- You'll need a Force.com organization.

 Note: Since this development scenario uses Visualforce, you can't use Database.com.

Accessing Data Using JavaScript

HTML5 apps require two static resource files, one for JQuery libraries and another for JavaScript remoting.

- The jQuery static resource contains all the JavaScript and stylesheet files for the jQuery and jQuery Mobile libraries.
- You'll also need a JavaScript file containing the methods that pull data from the Apex controller using JavaScript remoting. This data is then wrapped into appropriate HTML elements and rendered on the Visualforce page.

Take a look at the following JavaScript file.

```
function getAlbums(callback) {
    $j('#albumlist').empty();
    CloudtunesController.queryAlbums(function(records, e)
        { showAlbums(records, callback) }, {escape:true});
}
```

- In `getAlbums()`, calls such as `$j('#albumlist').empty()` are an indication of jQuery at work. In this case, jQuery retrieves the HTML element identified by `albumlist`, and clears out the HTML, readying it for results.
- The method then makes a call to the Apex controller's `queryAlbums()` method. This is where the JavaScript remoting magic happens. Visualforce provides all the required plumbing to allow the call to the controller method directly from the JavaScript.
- Finally, a callback function is passed as an argument to `queryAlbums()` that is automatically invoked once the records are returned from the Apex controller. The `showAlbums()` function takes these records and displays them.

Now let's take a look at showAlbums().

```javascript
function showAlbums(records, callback) {
    currentAlbums.length = 0;
    for(var i = 0; i < records.length; i++) {
        currentAlbums[records[i].Id] = records[i]; }

    $j.each(records, function() {
        $j('<li></li>')
        .attr('id',this.Id)
        .hide()
        .append('<h2>' + this.Name + '</h2>')
        .click(function(e) {
            e.preventDefault();
            $j.mobile.showPageLoadingMsg();
            $j('#AlbumName').html(currentAlbums[this.id].Name);
            $j('#AlbumPrice').html('$'+currentAlbums[this.id].Price__c);

            if($j('#AlbumPrice').html().indexOf(".") > 0
                    && $j('#AlbumPrice').html().split(".")[1].length -- 1)
    {
            $j('#AlbumPrice').html($j('#AlbumPrice').html()+"0"); //add
    trailing zero
        }
            $j('#AlbumId').val(currentAlbums[this.id].Id);
            var onTracksLoaded = function() {
            $j.mobile.hidePageLoadingMsg();
            $j.mobile.changePage('#detailpage', {changeHash: true});
        }
            getTracks(currentAlbums[this.id].Id, onTracksLoaded);
        })
        appendTo('#albumlist')
        .show();
        });

    $j('#albumlist').listview('refresh');
    if(callback != null && typeof callback == 'function') { callback();
    }
}
```

- This function gets the records from the callback, loops through them, and creates a new list of <li> HTML elements to display within the albumlist div.
- Notice this function also dynamically attaches a new event to each list item so that when the user clicks the list item, they can browse down to a list of tracks associated with the album. The list of those tracks is fetched using getTracks().

Now let's take a look at getTracks(). Functionally, this code is very similar to the getAlbums() and showAlbums() code. The only significant difference to the code that handled albums is that a different Apex controller method is used, and of course, a different callback function is provided for updating the page with the results.

```
function getTracks(albumid, callback) {
  $j('#tracklist').empty();
  CloudtunesController.queryTracks(albumid, function(records, e) {
    showTracks(records,callback) }, {escape:true} );
  return true;
}
```

Now anytime the album name is clicked, a new set of track data will be retrieved and the itemlist will be rewritten. Clicking on the track name will rewrite the HTML of the elements displaying the track information and use jQuery Mobile to move to that page. A real application can, of course, cache this information as well.

Chapter 9

Securely Storing Data Offline

Mobile devices can lose connection at any time, and environments such as hospitals and airplanes often prohibit connectivity. To handle these situations, it's important that your mobile apps continue to function when they go offline.

The Mobile SDK uses SmartStore, a secure offline storage solution on your device. SmartStore allows you to continue working even when the device is not connected to the Internet. SmartStore stores data as JSON documents in a data structure called a *soup*. A soup is a simple one-table database of "entries" which can be indexed in different ways and queried by a variety of methods.

 Note: Pure HTML5 apps store offline information in a browser cache. Browser caching isn't part of the Mobile SDK, and we don't document it here. SmartStore uses storage functionality on the device. This strategy requires a native or hybrid development path.

Sample Objects

The code snippets in this chapter use two objects, Account and Opportunity, which come predefined with every Salesforce organization. Account and Opportunity have a master-detail relationship; an Account can have more than one Opportunity.

Accessing SmartStore in Hybrid Apps

Hybrid containers access native device functionality, such as the camera, address book, and file storage, through JavaScript. SmartStore is also accessed from JavaScript. In order to enable offline access in a hybrid mobile application, you need to include a couple of JavaScript and CSS files in your Visualforce or HTML page.

- `cordova-1.8.1.js` — The Cordova library (formerly PhoneGap).
- `SFHybridApp.js` – Contains methods that perform utility tasks, such as determining whether you're offline.
- `SFSmartStorePlugin.js` – The core implementation of the SDK's offline functionality.

You store your offline data in SmartStore in one or more *soups*. A soup, conceptually speaking, is a logical collection of data records—represented as JSON objects—that you want to store and query offline. In the Force.com world, a soup will typically map to a standard or custom object that you wish to store offline, but that is not a hard and fast rule. You can store as many soups as you want in an application, but remember that soups are meant to be self-contained data sets; there is no direct correlation between them. In addition to storing the data itself, you can also specify indices that map to fields within the data, for greater ease and customization of data queries.

Note:

SmartStore data is inherently tied to the authenticated user. When the user logs out of the app, SmartStore deletes soup data associated with that user.

Offline Hybrid Development

Developing a hybrid application inside the container requires a build/deploy step for every change. For that reason, we recommend you develop your hybrid application directly in a browser, and only run your code in the container in the final stages of testing. JavaScript development in a browser is easier because there is no build/compile step. Whenever you make changes to the code, you can refresh the browser to see your changes.

We recommend using the Google Chrome browser because it comes bundled with developer tools that let you access the internals of the your web applications. For more information, see Chrome Developer Tools: Overview.

Using the Mock SmartStore

To facilitate developing and testing code that makes use of the SmartStore while running outside the container, you can use an emulated SmartStore. The MockSmartStore is a JavaScript implementation of the SmartStore that stores the data in local storage (or optionally just in memory).

 Note: The MockSmartStore doesn't encrypt data and is not meant to be used in production applications.

Inside the `PhoneGap` directory, there's a local directory containing the following files:

- `MockSmartStore.js` — A JavaScript implementation of the SmartStore meant only for development and testing outside the container.
- `MockSmartStorePlugin.js` A JavaScript helper class that intercepts SmartStore Cordova plugin calls and handles them using a MockSmartStore.
- `CordovaInterceptor.js` — A JavaScript helper class that intercepts Cordova plugin calls.

In your application's `index.html`, after your JavaScript include for `cordova-1.8.1.js` and `SFSmartStorePlugin.js`, add the following code to use the MockSmartStore.

```
$(function() {
    //Add event listener
    SFHybridApp.logToConsole("onLoad: jquery ready");
    document.addEventListener("deviceready", onDeviceReady,false);

    // Initialize mock smartstore
    // if true, use local storage, false, in memory only
    MockSmartStore.init(true);
    // Without a container, we have to do some  initialization
    cordova.completeInitalization();
});

    // When this function is called, Cordova has been initialized
    function onDeviceReady() {
        // that's where your application really starts
}
```

To see the MockSmartStore in action, check out `Cordova/local/test.html` in a browser.

Same-origin Policies

Same-origin policy permits scripts running on pages originating from the same site to access each other's methods and properties with no specific restrictions; it also blocks access to most methods and properties across pages on different sites. Same-origin policy restrictions are not an issue when your code runs inside the container, because the container disables same-origin policy in the webview. However, if you call a remote API, you need to worry about same-origin policy restrictions.

Fortunately, browsers offer ways to turn off same-origin policy, and you can research how to do that with your particular browser. If you want to make XHR calls against Force.com from JavaScript files loaded from the local file system, you should start your browser with same-origin policy disabled. The following article describes how to disable same-origin policy on several popular browsers: Getting Around Same-Origin Policy in Web Browsers.

Authentication

For authentication with MockSmartStore, you will need to capture access tokens and refresh tokens from a real session and hand code them in your JavaScript app. You'll also need these tokens to initialize the `ForceTk` JavaScript toolkit.

Registering a Soup

In order to access a soup, you first need to register it. Provide a name, index specifications, and names of callback functions for success and error conditions:

```
navigator.smartstore.registerSoup(soupName, indexSpecs, successCallback,
 errorCallback)
```

If the soup does not already exist, this function creates it. If the soup already exists, registering gives you access to the existing soup. To find out if a soup already exists, use:

```
navigator.smartstore.soupExists(soupName, successCallback,
errorCallback);
```

A soup is indexed on one or more fields found in its entries. Insert, update, and delete operations on soup entries are tracked in the soup indices. Always specify at least one index field when registering a soup. For example, if you are using the soup as a simple key/value store, use a single index specification with a string type.

indexSpecs

The `indexSpecs` array is used to create the soup with predefined indexing. Entries in the `indexSpecs` array specify how the soup should be indexed. Each entry consists of a `path:type` pair. `path` is the name of an index field; `type` is either "string" or "integer". Index paths are case-sensitive and can include compound paths, such as Owner.Name.

Note: Performance can suffer if the index path is too deep. If index entries are missing any fields described in a particular `indexSpec`, they will not be tracked in that index.

```
"indexSpecs":[
    {
        "path":"Name",
        "type":"string"
    }
    {
        "path":"Id",
        "type":"string"
    }
    {
        "path":"ParentId",
        "type":"string"
    }
    {
        "path":"lastModifiedDate",
        "type":"integer"
    }
]
```

 Note: Currently, the Mobile SDK supports two index types: "string" and "integer." These types apply only to the index itself, and not to the way data is stored or retrieved. It's OK to have a null field in an index column.

successCallback

The success callback function for `registerSoup` takes one argument (the soup name).

```
function(soupName) { alert("Soup " + soupName + " was successfully
created"); };
```

A successful creation of the soup returns a `successCallback` that indicates the soup is ready. Wait to complete the transaction and receive the callback before you begin any activity. If you register a soup under the passed name, the success callback function returns the soup.

errorCallback

The error callback function for `registerSoup` takes one argument (the error description string).

```
function(err) { alert ("registerSoup failed with error:" + err); }
```

During soup creation, errors can happen for a number of reasons, including:

- An invalid or bad soup name
- No index (at least one index must be specified)

- Other unexpected errors, such as a database error

Retrieving Data From a Soup

SmartStore provides a set of helper methods that build query strings for you. To query a specific set of records, call the `build*` method that suits your query specification. You can optionally define the index field, sort order, and other metadata to be used for filtering, as described in the following table:

Parameter	Description
indexPath	This is what you're searching for; for example a name, account number, or date.
beginKey	Optional. Used to define the start of a range query.
endKey	Optional. Used to define the end of a range query.
order	Optional. Either "ascending" or "descending."
pageSize	Optional. If not present, the native plugin can return whatever page size it sees fit in the resulting `Cursor.pageSize`.

Note:

All queries are single-predicate searches. Queries don't support joins.

Query Everything

`buildAllQuerySpec(indexPath, order, [pageSize])` returns all entries in the soup, with no particular order. Use this query to traverse everything in the soup.

`order` and `pageSize` are optional, and default to ascending and 10, respectively. You can specify:

- `buildAllQuerySpec(indexPath)`
- `buildAllQuerySpec(indexPath, order)`
- `buildAllQuerySpec(indexPath, order, [pageSize])`

However, you can't specify `buildAllQuerySpec(indexPath, [pageSize])`.

See Working With Cursors for information on page sizes.

Note: As a base rule, set `pageSize` to the number of entries you want displayed on the screen. For a smooth scrolling display, you might want to increase the value to two or three times the number of entries actually shown.

Query by Exact

`buildExactQuerySpec(indexPath, matchKey, [pageSize])` finds entries that exactly match the given `matchKey` for the `indexPath` value. Use this to find child entities of a given ID. For example, you can find Opportunities by Status. However, you can't specify order in the results.

Sample code for retrieving children by ID:

```
var querySpec = navigator.smartstore.buildExactQuerySpec("sfdcId",
"some-sfdc-id");
navigator.smartstore.querySoup("Catalogs", querySpec, function(cursor)
{
     // we expect the catalog to be in:
cursor.currentPageOrderedEntries[0]
});
```

Sample code for retrieving children by parent ID:

```
var querySpec = navigator.smartstore.buildExactQuerySpec("parentSfdcId",
 "some-sfdc-id);
navigator.smartstore.querySoup("Catalogs", querySpec, function(cursor)
 {});
```

Query by Range

`buildRangeQuerySpec(indexPath, beginKey, endKey, [order, pageSize])` finds entries whose `indexPath` values fall into the range defined by `beginKey` and `endKey`. Use this function to search by numeric ranges, such as a range of dates stored as integers.

`order` and `pageSize` are optional, and default to ascending and 10, respectively. You can specify:

- `buildRangeQuerySpec(indexPath, beginKey, endKey)`
- `buildRangeQuerySpec(indexPath, beginKey, endKey, order)`
- `buildRangeQuerySpec(indexPath, beginKey, endKey, order, pageSize)`

However, you can't specify `buildRangeQuerySpec(indexPath, beginKey, endKey, pageSize)`.

By passing null values to `beginKey` and `endKey`, you can perform open-ended searches:

- Passing `null` to `endKey` finds all records where the field at `indexPath` is `>= beginKey`.
- Passing `null` to `beginKey` finds all records where the field at `indexPath` is `<= endKey`.

- Passing `null` to both `beginKey` and `endKey` is the same as querying everything.

Query by Like

`buildLikeQuerySpec(indexPath, likeKey, [order, pageSize])` finds entries whose `indexPath` values are like the given `likeKey`. You can use "foo%" to search for terms that begin with your keyword, "%foo" to search for terms that end with your keyword, and "%foo%" to search for your keyword anywhere in the `indexPath` value. Use this function for general searching and partial name matches. `order` and `pageSize` are optional, and default to ascending and 10, respectively.

 Note: Query by Like is the slowest of the query methods.

Executing the Query

Queries run asynchronously and return a cursor to your JavaScript callback. Your success callback should be of the form `function(cursor)`. Use the `querySpec` parameter to pass your query specification to the `querySoup` method.

```
navigator.smartstore.querySoup(soupName,querySpec,successCallback,errorCallback);
```

Retrieving Individual Soup Entries by Primary Key

All soup entries are automatically given a unique internal ID (the primary key in the internal table that holds all entries in the soup). That ID field is made available as the `_soupEntryId` field in the soup entry. Soup entries can be looked up by `_soupEntryId` by using the `retrieveSoupEntries` method. Note that the return order is not guaranteed, and if entries have been deleted they will be missing from the resulting array. This method provides the fastest way to retrieve a soup entry, but it's usable only when you know the `_soupEntryId`:

```
navigator.smartStore.retrieveSoupEntries(soupName, indexSpecs,
successCallback, errorCallback)
```

Working With Cursors

Queries can potentially have long result sets that are too large to load. Instead, only a small subset of the query results (a single page) is copied from the native realm to the JavaScript realm at any given time. When you perform a query, a cursor object is returned from the native realm that provides a way to page through a list of query results. The JavaScript code can then move forward and back through the pages, causing pages to be copied to the JavaScript realm.

Note: For advanced users: Cursors are not snapshots of data; they are dynamic. If you make changes to the soup and then start paging through the cursor, you will see those changes. The only data the cursor holds is the original query and your current position in the result set. When you move your cursor, the query runs again. Thus, newly created soup entries can be returned (assuming they satisfy the original query).

Use the following cursor functions to navigate the results of a query:

- `navigator.smartstore.moveCursorToPageIndex(cursor, newPageIndex, successCallback, errorCallback)`—Move the cursor to the page index given, where 0 is the first page, and the last page is defined by `totalPages - 1`.
- `navigator.smartstore.moveCursorToNextPage(cursor, successCallback, errorCallback)`—Move to the next entry page if such a page exists.
- `navigator.smartstore.moveCursorToPreviousPage(cursor, successCallback, errorCallback)`—Move to the previous entry page if such a page exists.
- `navigator.smartstore.closeCursor(cursor, successCallback, errorCallback)`—Close the cursor when you're finished with it.

Note: `successCallback` for those functions should expect one argument (the updated cursor).

Manipulating Data

In order to track soup entries for insert, update, and delete, the SmartStore adds a few fields to each entry:

- `_soupEntryId`—This field is the primary key for the soup entry in the table for a given soup.
- `_soupLastModifiedDate`—The number of milliseconds since 1/1/1970.
    - ◊ To convert to a JavaScript date, use `new Date(entry._soupLastModifiedDate)`
    - ◊ To convert a date to the corresponding number of milliseconds since 1/1/1970, use `date.getTime()`

When inserting or updating soup entries, SmartStore automatically sets these fields. When removing or retrieving specific entries, you can reference them by `_soupEntryId`.

Inserting or Updating Soup Entries

If the provided soup entries already have the _soupEntryId slots set, then entries identified by that slot are updated in the soup. If an entry does not have a _soupEntryId slot, or the value of the slot doesn't match any existing entry in the soup, then the entry is added (inserted) to the soup, and the _soupEntryId slot is overwritten.

 Note: You must not manipulate the _soupEntryId or _soupLastModifiedDate value yourself.

Use the upsertSoupEntries method to insert or update entries:

```
navigator.smartStore.upsertSoupEntries(soupName, entries[],
successCallback, errorCallback)
```

where soupName is the name of the target soup, and entries is an array of one or more entries that match the soup's data structure. The successCallback and errorCallback parameters function much like the ones for registerSoup. However, the success callback for upsertSoupEntries indicates that either a new record has been inserted, or an existing record has been updated.

Upserting with an External ID

If your soup entries mirror data from an external system, you might need to refer to those entities by their ID (primary key) in the external system. For that purpose, we support upsert with an external ID. When you perform an upsert, you can designate any index field as the external ID field. SmartStore will look for existing soup entries with the same value in the designated field with the following results:

- If no field with the same value is found, a new soup entry will be created.
- If the external ID field is found, it will be updated.
- If more than one field matches the external ID, an error will be returned.

When creating a new entry locally, use a regular upsert. Set the external ID field to a value that you can later query when uploading the new entries to the server.

When updating entries with data coming from the server, use the upsert with external ID. Doing so guarantees that you don't end up with duplicate soup entries for the same remote entity.

In the following sample code, we chose the value new for the id field because the record doesn't yet exist on the server. Once we are online, we can query for records that exist only locally (by looking for records where id == "new") and upload them to the server. Once the server returns the actual ID for the records, we can update their id fields locally. If you create products that belong to catalogs that have not yet been created on the server, you will be able to capture the relationship with the catalog through the `parentSoupEntryId` field. Once the catalogs are created on the server, update the local records' `parentExternalId` fields.

The following code contains sample scenarios. First, it calls `upsertSoupEntries` to create a new soup entry. In the success callback, the code retrieves the new record with its newly assigned soup entry ID. It then changes the description and calls `ForceTK` methods to create the new account on the server and then update it. The final call demonstrates the upsert with external ID. To make the code more readable, no error callbacks are specified. Also, because all SmartStore calls are asynchronous, real applications should do each step in the callback of the previous step.

```
// Specify data for the account to be created
var acc = {id: "new", Name: "Cloud Inc", Description:
  "Getting started"};

// Create account in SmartStore
// This upsert does a create because the acc has no _soupEntryId field
navigator.smartstore.upsertSoupEntries("accounts", [ acc ],
function(accounts) {
    acc = accounts[0];
    // acc should now have a _soupEntryId field and _lastModifiedDate
});

// Update account's description in memory
acc["Description"] = "Just shipped our first app ";

// Update account in SmartStore
// This does an "update" because acc has a _soupEntryId field
navigator.smartstore.upsertSoupEntries("accounts", [ acc ],
function(accounts) {
    acc = accounts[0];
});

// Create account on server
forcetkClient.create("account", {"Name": acc["Name"], "Description":
acc["Description"]}, function(result) {
    acc["id"] = result["id"];
    // Update account in SmartStore
    Navigator.smartstore.upsertSoupEntries("accounts", [ acc ]);
});

// Update account's description in memory
acc["Description"] = "Now shipping for iOS and Android";

// Update account's description on server
// Sync client -> server for entities existing on server
forcetkClient.update("account", acc["id"], {"Description":
acc["Description"]});

// Later, there is an account (id: someSfdcId) you want to get locally

// There might be an older version in the SmartStore already
```

```
// Update account on client
// sync server/client for entities that might not exist on client
forcetkClient.retrieve("account", someSfdcId, "id,Name,Description",
function(result) {
    // Create or update account in SmartStore
    Navigator.smartstore.upsertSoupEntriesWithExternalId("accounts",
      [ result ], "id");
});
```

Removing Soup Entries

Entries are removed from the soup asynchronously and your callback is called with success or failure. The `soupEntryIds` is a list of the `_soupEntryId` values from the entries you wish to delete.

```
navigator.smartStore.removeFromSoup(soupName, soupEntryIds,
successCallback, errorCallback)
```

Removing a Soup

To remove a soup, call `removeSoup()`. Note that once a user signs out, the soups get deleted automatically.

```
navigator.smartstore.removeSoup(soupName,successCallback,errorCallback);
```

SmartStore Extensions

Some apps might profit by extending the SmartStore API in various ways.

- Secure localStorage—W3C's `localStorage` is a simple key-value storage that can be readily implemented on top of SmartStore. For instance, a single `localStorage` soup can be created by the SmartStore plugin on each platform, and the `matchKey` can be the key passed to the `localStorage` methods. This is a convenience layer for developers who are already familiar with `localStorage` and comfortable with its limitations. The main difference in our implementation is the need to rely on Cordova-style JavaScript callbacks, so all `localStorage` methods are asynchronous.
- Files and Large Binary Objects—Some apps require the ability to store large binary objects, such as video, PDF, and PPT files. For these apps, there is currently no consistent secure storage mechanism in Cordova.

Chapter 10

Advanced Topics

In this chapter ...

- Customize the Hybrid Sample App to Use the Camera
- Bar Code and QR Code Scanning
- Geolocation and Mobile Apps
- Utilizing Near Field Communication (NFC) in Hybrid Apps

The previous chapters focused on getting your basic app built, with some additional tweaks that show you how to get the sample applications do what you want. By this time you can probably create projects, build apps, and modify the sample apps to work with your own organization and its data. The following sections help you continue to build out your app by adding additional functionality in the device.

Customize the Hybrid Sample App to Use the Camera

This section shows you how hybrid apps can access the native features of the device, specifically the camera. To get you started quickly, we've provided a sample project.

1. Point your browser to GitHub and download the GlueCon 2012 Salesforce Mobile SDK Demo project into a new directory:

```
git clone
https://github.com/metadaddy-sfdc/GlueCon2012-Salesforce-Mobile-SDK-Demo.git
```

2. Copy the files and images from `GlueCon2012-Salesforce-Mobile-SDK-Demo/www` directory into your hybrid app's `www` directory, overwriting `forcetk.js`, `index.html` and `inline.js`, and creating a new `images` folder.

Before you run the app, you'll need to make a couple of customizations to the Contact standard object in your DE org. You'll need to create one custom field to hold the image ID, and another to display the image on the Contact Page Layout. The app uploads images to ContentVersion records, and updates the Contact record with the new ContentVersion record's ID.

1. Log in to your DE account and select **Your Name** > **Setup** > **App Setup** > **Customize** > **Contacts** > **Fields**.
2. Scroll down to **Contact Custom Fields & Relationships** and click **New**.
3. Select **Text** as the field type and click **Next**.
4. On the following screen, enter:

   - **Field Label:** Image ID
   - **Length:** 18

5. Click **Next**, then click **Next** again to accept the field-level security defaults. On the next screen, deselect all of the page layouts and click **Save & New**.

    Note: The image field should be visible to the user, but the image ID... not so much. By deselecting the ID field here, it won't be added to the page layout.

You're going to create another field, but this one is based on a formula.

1. Select **Formula** as the field type and click **Next**.
2. On the following screen, enter:

   - **Field Label:** Image

- **Formula Return Type:** Text

3. Click **Next** and enter the following formula.

```
IF( Image_ID__c != null ,
    IMAGE( '/sfc/servlet.shepherd/version/download/' &
Image_ID__c, '') ,
    IMAGE('' , '' , 0 , 0))
```

4. Click **Next**, then click **Next** again to accept the field-level security defaults, and click **Save** to accept the page layout defaults.

 Note: This time the image field should be displayed on all page layouts.

Run the App

Now that you've configured your project and the Contacts standard object, you're ready to run the demo app and upload images to contacts!

 Note: There is no camera in the iOS simulator, so you'll need to run this on a physical device.

1. Launch the app, login if necessary, and click **Fetch SFDC contacts**.
2. In the demo app, you can click a contact in the list to access a contact detail page, including a placeholder for a photo of the contact.

3. Tap the placeholder image and the camera will activate.
4. Take a picture, and the contact detail page will be updated with the image, the image data will be uploaded to a ContentVersion record, and associated with the contact.

5. To verify that this really worked, log into your DE org.
6. Click the **Contacts** tab, you'll see the contact in the **Recent Contacts** list.
7. Click on the contact and you'll see the photo alongside the standard Contact data.

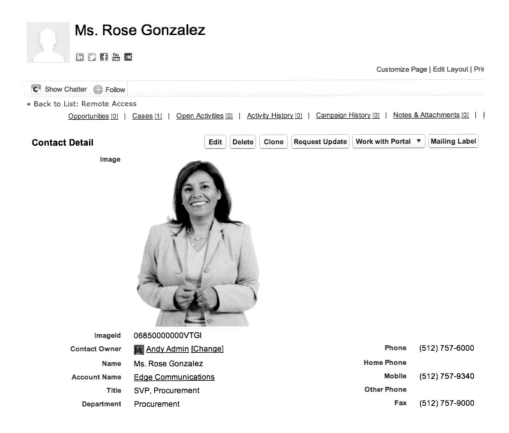

How the Demo App Works

Take a look at index.html and inline.js, and you'll see a number of differences from the sample app. The device contacts and accounts lists have been removed from index.html, and there is a new 'Contact Detail' page comprising an image and Name, Account Name and Phone Number fields.

In inline.js, look at onSuccessSfdcContactList() first.

```
function onSuccessSfdcContactList(response) {
    var $j = jQuery.noConflict();

    SFHybridApp.logToConsole("onSuccessSfdcContactList: received " +

            response.totalSize + " contacts");

    $j("#div_sfdc_contact_list").html("")
    var ul = $j('<ul data-role="listview" data-inset="true"
data-theme="a" data-dividertheme="a"></ul>');
    $j("#div_sfdc_contact_list").append(ul);
```

```
   ul.append($j('<li data-role="list-divider">Salesforce Contacts: '
+
           response.totalSize + '</li>'));
   $j.each(response.records, function(i, contact) {
      var id = contact.Id;
      var newLi = $j("<li><a href='#'>" + (i+1) + " - " + contact.Name
+ "</a></li>");
       newLi.click(function(e){
           e.preventDefault();
           $j.mobile.showPageLoadingMsg();
           forcetkClient.query("SELECT Id, Name, Account.Name, Phone,
Image_ID__c "+
                   "FROM Contact WHERE Id = '"+id+"'",
                   onSuccessSfdcSingleContact, onErrorSfdc);
       });
       ul.append(newLi);
   });

   $j("#div_sfdc_contact_list").trigger( "create" )
}
```

For each record passed in, within the response we create a list item with its name, and set up a click handler on the list item to retrieve the contact's name, account name, phone number, and image.

The query callback, onSuccessSfdcSingleContact(), populates the contact detail page. Notice the code to display the contact image.

```
//Set up image
$j('#Image').attr('data-id', contact.Id);
$j('#Image').attr('data-name', contact.Name);
if (contact.Image_ID__c) {
   // Load image data
   $j('#Image').attr('src', "images/loading.png");

   $j.mobile.changePage('#jqm-detail');

   forcetkClient.retrieveBlobField("ContentVersion",
           contact.Image_ID__c, "VersionData", function(response) {
       var base64data = base64ArrayBuffer(response);
      $j('#Image').attr('src', "data:image/png;base64,"+base64data);

       $j.mobile.hidePageLoadingMsg();
   }, onErrorSfdc);
} else {
   // Display a default image
   $j.mobile.hidePageLoadingMsg();
   $j('#Image').attr('src', "images/blank.png");
   $j.mobile.changePage('#jqm-detail');
}
```

The contact ID and name are set as attributes on the image element, and, if there is an ID in the `Image_ID__c` custom field, a 'loading' image is displayed, and the image data is retrieved via `retrieveBlobField()`.

The `base64ArrayBuffer()` utility function converts the JavaScript `ArrayBuffer` object to base64-encoded data as a string, and the callback sets the image data as a data URI.

Looking at `regLinkClickHandlers()`, this function loses the `#link_fetch_device_contacts` and `#link_fetch_sfdc_accountshandlers`, but gains a new one:

```
$j('#Image').click(function() {
    getPhotoAndUploadToContact($j(this).attr('data-name'),
        $j(this).attr('data-id'));
});
```

Clicking the image calls the `getPhotoAndUploadToContact()` function, passing in the contact name and ID attributes from the image element.

```
function getPhotoAndUploadToContact(name, contactId) {
    SFHybridApp.logToConsole("in capturePhoto, contactId = "+contactId);

    $j('#Image').attr('data-old-src', $j('#Image').attr('src'));
    $j('#Image').attr('src', "images/camera.png");

    navigator.camera.getPicture(function(imageData){
        onPhotoDataSuccess(imageData, name, contactId);
    }, function(errorMsg){
        // Most likely error is user cancelling out of camera
        $j('#dialog-text').html(errorMsg);
        $j.mobile.changePage('#jqm-dialog');
        $j('#Image').attr('src', $j('#Image').attr('data-old-src'));
        $j('#Image').removeAttr('data-old-src');
    }, {
        quality: 50,
        sourceType: Camera.PictureSourceType.CAMERA,
        destinationType: Camera.DestinationType.DATA_URL
    });
}
```

`getPhotoAndUploadToContact()` really shows the power of the hybrid approach. The `getPicture()` function on`navigator.camera` provides easy access to the device camera. The options passed to `getPicture()` specify the required image quality, source (camera in this case, as opposed to the device's photo library), and the format in which the picture should be returned. `Camera.DestinationType.DATA_URL` returns the image as a base64-encoded string, while `Camera.DestinationType.FILE_URI` returns a URI to a file on the device.

When a picture is successfully taken, the `onPhotoDataSuccess()` callback is invoked.

```
function onPhotoDataSuccess(imageData, name, contactId) {
    var $j = jQuery.noConflict();

    SFHybridApp.logToConsole("in onPhotoDataSuccess, contactId =
"+contactId);

    // Update the image on screen
    $j('#Image').attr('src', "data:image/jpeg;base64," + imageData);

    // Upload the image data to Content
    $j.mobile.showPageLoadingMsg();
    forcetkClient.create('ContentVersion', {
        "PathOnClient" : name + ".png",
        "VersionData" : imageData
    }, function(data){
        // Now update the Contact record with the new ContentVersion
Id
        SFHybridApp.logToConsole('Created ContentVersion ' + data.id);

        forcetkClient.update('Contact', contactId, {
            "Image_ID__c" : data.id
        }, function(){
            $j.mobile.hidePageLoadingMsg();
            SFHybridApp.logToConsole('Updated Contact '+contactId);
        }, onErrorSfdc);
    }, onErrorSfdc);
}
```

After updating the on-screen image, a `ContentVersion` record is created. Note that we indicate the type of the data via the extension on the `PathOnClient` field. On successful creation, the contact is updated with the ID of the new `ContentVersion` record.

Bar Code and QR Code Scanning

Hybrid apps fall somewhere in between the web and native spectrum of mobile development. Like web apps, hybrid mobile apps are developed primarily in web technologies like HTML5, JavaScript, and CSS. However, you can then use the Salesforce Mobile SDK container (which is based on the open source PhoneGap project) to put a thin native 'wrapper' around the web application and access native device features like the camera, microphone, etc. Hybrid applications can access native device capabilities – the ability to snap a picture on the mobile device and attach it to the respective Merchandise record in Salesforce. Another common use case for developing Hybrid applications is scanning bar codes or QR codes.

So how does one go about adding support for bar code scanning in a Hybrid mobile application? This is where the beauty of the PhoneGap (aka Apache Cordova) hybrid framework shines through. PhoneGap has a rich 'plugin' library of open source components built by the community to support advanced use cases like push notification, mobile payments (using PayPal) and yes, bar code and QR Code scanning. In fact, the Salesforce Mobile SDK itself uses PhoneGap plugins to support our OAuth login process and our secure offline storage (aka SmartStore).

Let's say we wanted to enhance our MerchandiseMobile Visualforce page to allow users to search for Merchandise records by scanning a bar code or QR Code. You can peruse the final codebase for this application in GitHub, but here are the step-by-step instructions for adding bar code scanning to your Hybrid mobile application.

1. Convert your Visualforce page into a Hybrid application using the Salesforce Mobile SDK. Detailed instructions on how you can do this can be found in Tutorials 5 (iOS) and 6 (Android) of the Mobile SDK workbook.

2. Download the GitHub repo for the PhoneGap plugins to your local machine (using git clone or clicking the 'Downloads' link on the top right). Depending on which mobile platform you're developing for, follow the instructions in the readme file to import the bar code scanner plugin in your Android or iOS project.

3. Import the barcodescanner.js file that is included in the PhoneGap plugin Git repo into your Visualforce page. For example, here is a small snippet from my MerchandiseMobile VF page.

```
<apex:includeScript
value="{!URLFOR($Resource.BarCodeScanner)}"/>
```

 Note: You also need to import the core PhoneGap JS file in your Visualforce page.

4. We're now ready to initiate bar code scanning from our Visualforce page. The great thing about PhoneGap is that you can access all device functions via JavaScript – no

iOS/Android specific coding required. Here is how to invoke the Bar Code scanner PhoneGap plugin in the Visualforce page.

```
function scanBarCode() {
    window.plugins.barcodeScanner.scan(onBarcodeScanSuccess,
 onBarcodeScanFailure);
}

function onBarcodeScanSuccess(result) {
    MerchandiseMobileController.getMerchandiseRecByBarCode(
                result.text,
                function(res,event){
                    if (res != null){
                        $j.mobile.showPageLoadingMsg();

$j('#merchandiseName').html(res.Name);

$j('#description').html(res.Description__c);

$j('#inventory').html(res.Total_Inventory__c);
                        $j('#price').html('$'+res.Price__c);

                        $j('#merchandiseId').val(res.Id);
                        $j.mobile.hidePageLoadingMsg();

                        $j.mobile.changePage('#detailpage',
 {changeHash: true});
                    }
                    else{
                        alert('Sorry. No matching
Merchandise records found.');
                    }
                });
}

function onBarcodeScanFailure(error) {
    console.log("Barcode scanning failed: " + error);
}
```

Line 2 shows how simple it is to use bar code scanning using the custom PhoneGap plugin. If the bar code/QR code scan is successful, the success callback function gets invoked with the scanned text or string ('result.text' above). The plugin also passes along the format of the bar code scanned (e.g. 'QR_CODE', 'UPC_A', 'DATA_MATRIX' etc.) via the 'result.format' variable. Then simply use JavaScript Remoting to invoke a method on the Apex controller attached to this VF page (line 6) to search for any Merchandise records that match the scanned bar code value.

In addition to using the hybrid approach described above, you can also implement bar code scanning in a native mobile application if you're comfortable with native Android or iOS development.

Geolocation and Mobile Apps

The composite field type, geolocation, consists of two components: longitude and latitude. It is specifically designed to hold the geo-coordinates of a location for any objects, most commonly address related objects, such as Contact, Account, restaurants, shops, etc. When a geolocation field is added to these objects, and coordinates are set, users can perform radius-based searches. Some examples: to find the records of restaurants within 5 miles of the current location, to find all the homes within 15 miles of a sports arena, etc.

Mobile applications find this new feature especially handy for providing mobile location-based search on Salesforce objects. Just like a regular custom field type, the geolocation field can be added to an object through the object setup wizard. During setup you can set the decimal point precision, which allows users to display coordinates in decimal point or degree-minute-second notations.

 Note: This is a beta release of geolocation and its functionality has known limitations, outlined here. To provide feedback on geolocation, go to IdeaExchange.

Creating a Geolocation Custom Field

1. Click **Your Name** > **Setup** > **Create** > **ObjectsCreate** > **Objects** and select one of the custom objects in the list.
2. In Custom Fields & Relationships, click **New**.
3. Choose **Geolocation** and click **Next**.
4. Enter the Geolocation field attributes, including Latitude and Longitude Display Notation , which determines how the notation appears in the Salesforce interface:

   Degrees, Minutes, Seconds

   > A notation for angular measurement that is based on the number 60: there are 360 degrees to a circle, 60 minutes to a degree, and 60 seconds to a minute.

   Decimal

   > Expresses the value as degrees, and converts the minutes and seconds to a decimal fraction of the degree. Decimal notation does not use cardinal points. North and East are positive values; South and West are negative values.

5. Follow the steps to complete the wizard.

Radius-based Searching and Filtering

List views for objects with a geolocation field have a `WITHIN` operator to conduct radius based searching and filtering. You can perform distance calculation between two geolocation points using the `DISTANCE(loc1, loc2, distance_unit)` function inside formula fields.

Also, SOQL is enhanced with `DISTANCE` and `GEOLOCATION` functions, which lets you write SOQL queries to perform location-based searches. For example, the geo coordinates of 1 Market Street, San Francisco, California are 37.794915,-122.394733. To find the names and phone numbers of all restaurants within 1 mile, you can write a SOQL query as:

```
SELECT name__c, phone__c
  FROM restaurant__c
 WHERE DISTANCE(loc__c, GEOLOCATION(37.794915,-122.394733), "mi") <=
1
```

Geolocation Field Limitations

Geolocation is a compound field that counts toward your organization's limits as three custom fields: one for latitude, one for longitude, and one for internal use. In this beta release, support for the compound field (geolocation) vs. the field's components (latitude and longitude) varies depending on the functionality you're using in Salesforce. For example, you can create list views that show the field and its components, but you can't select the compound geolocation field in Apex; you can only run SOQL queries on a geolocation field's components.

Other limitations of this geolocation beta release include:

- History tracking is not available for geolocation fields.
- Geolocation fields are not supported in custom settings.
- Geolocation fields are not available in reports, dashboards, validation rules, Visual Workflow, or workflow and approvals.
- Geolocation fields cannot be searched.
- Geolocation fields are not available in Schema Builder.
- DISTANCE and GEOLOCATION formula functions are available only when creating formula fields and in Visual Workflow.
- Geolocation is supported in Apex only through SOQL queries, and only at the component level.

Utilizing Near Field Communication (NFC) in Hybrid Apps

Imagine walking a conference floor, having the ability to instantly and effortlessly upload any business card you receive into your Salesforce org as a full blown Contact record. You don't need to open an application on your smartphone and take a QR code picture. You don't need to take a picture of the card and type in the information later. You just tap the business card to your smartphone and it's instantly uploaded into Salesforce. You can do this with the Salesforce Touch Platform and a near field communications-enabled device.

NFC stands for Near Field Communication. It allows devices to exchange data wirelessly at very short ranges (less than a few centimeters). Devices that can transmit data via NFC are called "tags." Tags can come in varying physical shapes and sizes, such as round stickers, business cards, credit cards, or nametags. They also come in a variety of data sizes, holding as little as a few bytes to up to four Kilobytes or more. As you might expect, the data on tags can be encoded in a variety of formats. That being said, there is one format that is widely used called NDEF (NFC Data Exchange Format). Formatting a tag in NDEF format allows an easy exchange of the tag data with systems that leverage the format. For example, Android devices support the NDEF format and are the easiest format to get started with.

Requirements

You need to ensure you have a mobile device that supports NFC if you want to execute this application in the wild. You can get a list of Android NFC phones online by searching for "NFC Smartphones." You'll also need some NFC tags to work with. Again, you can Google for NFC tags and get a list of retailers who sell blank or NDEF-formatted tags. Getting the tags NDEF formatted from the retailer makes it somewhat easier to encode your data. Also, ensure you review the size of data the NFC tag can hold. Depending on your needs, you might want a tag with more data capacity.

Note that there are some software NFC emulators available for downloading if you don't have the hardware. Software emulators are not covered here.

Force.com and NFC Mobile Application Architecture

If you just want to follow along and not get your hands dirty building this yourself, download the source code for they hybrid Android app from the NFC vCard Cloud Loader app: `https://github.com/corycowgill/NFC_vCard_Loader`.

One great thing about PhoneGap is its plugin architecture. The PhoneGap framework allows developers to create plugins that utilize hardware in a device and return data from those devices to mobile applications HTML via JavaScript. Since NFC is dependent on native API calls to the device, the app uses an open source NFC PhoneGap plugin created by Don Coleman at Chariot Solutions. You can get the NFC Plugin on his Github site `https://github.com/chariotsolutions/phonegap-nfc`.

Installing the NFC PhoneGap Plugin

Installing a PhoneGap plugin is a fairly easy and straightforward process. There are only a few things you need to do.

1. Download `phonegap-nfc-android.jar` from `https://github.com/chariotsolutions/phonegap-nfc/downloads` and the JavaScript file (`phonegap-nfc.js`) for the plugin.

2. Copy the JAR file for the Plugin into your application's library folder and ensure the JAR file is on your application's classpath.

3. Copy the JavaScript file (`phonegap-nfc.js`) into your application's JavaScript folder.

4. Update your HTML files to include the plugins JavaScript file.

```
<script type="text/javascript"

src="[view-source:https://dl-web.dropbox.com/get/SalesforceMobileSDK-Android/

hybrid/SampleApps/ContactExplorer/assets/www/phonegap-nfc-0.2.0.js

        phonegap-nfc-0.2.0.js] script>
```

5. Update your PhoneGap plugin xml file (plugins.xml) to include the plugin class:

```
<plugin name="NfcPlugin"
value="com.chariotsolutions.nfc.plugin.NfcPlugin"/>
```

6. Update your Android Manifest file to allow the application device permission to use NFC:

```
<uses-permission android:name="android.permission.NFC" />
```

7. *Optional* – Android has a special notification system for NFC tags. The NFC Tag Dispatcher runs in the background of Android and can be configured to automatically start an application once a device scans an NFC tag. This allows your application to instantly fire when an NFC tag is read. To do this, update your Android Manifest with the proper intent tags:

```
<intent-filter>
  <action android:name="android.nfc.action.NDEF_DISCOVERED"/>
  <data android:mimeType="text/pg" />
  <category android:name="android.intent.category.DEFAULT" />
</intent-filter>
```

That is everything you need to do to configure your workspace and application for NFC. Now, let's take a look at the application code.

Invoking the NFC Plugin via JavaScript

NFC functionality is event-driven. As such, you need to have your application listen for the NFC tag scans fired from the Android Tag Dispatcher and then execute logic. The NFC PhoneGap Plugin handles the heavy lifting for processing the NFC tag read events. You just need to register listeners in the JavaScript to process the callbacks from the NFC Plugin. To do this, you register the NFC listeners for the plugin object inside the device-ready method of PhoneGap:

```
// When this function is called, PhoneGap is initialized
    function onDeviceReady() {
        SFHybridApp.logToConsole("onDeviceReady: PhoneGap ready");
    //Call getAuthCredentials to get the initial session credentials

SalesforceOAuthPlugin.getAuthCredentials(salesforceSessionRefreshed,

            ge-tAuthCredentialsError);

        //receive notifications when autoRefreshOnForeground refreshes
    the session
        docu-ment.addEventListener("salesforceSessionRefresh",
            salesforceSessionRefreshed,false);

        //enable buttons
        reqLinkClickHandlers();

        //Use the NFC Plugin to configure the NFC Tag Reader Listener

        nfc.addNdefListener(
            onNfcRead,
                successNFCRegisterListener,
                errorNFCRegisterListener
    );

    regLinkNFCClickHandlers();

    }
```

As you can see above, you specify the callback handler (onNfcRead) to process the tag data returned from the NFC tag. You also have two additional callback methods specified: `successNFCRegisterListener` and `errorNFCRegisterListener`. Those methods execute once the listener is successfully register in our JavaScript.

You can specify in the JavaScript how to handle the results of a NFC tag. The code below displays the NFC tag data on the screen when it's scanned. Then parse the tag data, formatted in vCard format, and store it in a contact variable. This contact variable eventually passes to the Mobile SDK to be inserted into Salesforce.

```
function onNfcRead(nfcEvent) {
    console.log(JSON.stringify(nfcEvent.tag)); // Debug in Console
    clearScreen(); // Clear Previosly Display Tag Info
    var tag = nfcEvent.tag;
    var records = tag.ndefMessage || [],
    //Tag Content HTML Div
    display = document.getElementById("tagContents");
    display.appendChild(
        document.createTextNode(
            "Scanned an NDEF tag with " + records.length +
            " record" + ((re-cords.length === 1) ? "": "s")
        )
    );

    // Display Tag Info
    var meta = document.createElement('dl');
    display.appendChild(meta);

    if (device.platform.match(/Android/i)) {
        if (tag.id) {
            showProperty(meta, "Id", nfc.bytesToHexString(tag.id));
        }
        var hcard = document.createElement("div");
    hcard.innerHTML =
vCard.initialize(nfc.bytesToString(tag.ndefMessage[0].payload)).to_html();

        display.appendChild(hcard);
    var vCardVal =
vCard.initialize(nfc.bytesToString(tag.ndefMessage[0].payload));
//parse the Tag formatted vCard data into a Javascript Object
    var names = vCardVal.fn.split(" ");//Take Fullname from vCard
    contact.firstName = names[0]; //Put in Firstname for SFDC
    contact.lastName = names[1]; //Put in LastName for SFDC
    for(type in vCardVal.email)
        {
          for(n in vCardVal.email['home'])
          {
            //Store email in contact variable for SFDC Upsert
                  contact.email = vCardVal.email['home'][n];
            contact.vCard_Email__c = contact.email;
          }
        }
        for(type in vCardVal.tel)
        {
          for(n in vCardVal.tel[type])
          {
                  //Store Telephone Info in variable for SFDC Upsert
            contact.phone = vCardVal.tel[type][n];
          }
        }
     meta.appendChild(hcard);
    }
```

```
        navigator.notification.vibrate(100);
    }
```

As you can see in the above code, the JavaScript processes the returned NDEF tag payload from the NFC plugin. You then parse the tag information, format in vCard format, and append it to the DOM. The information then renders on the screen to the user. If you are unfamiliar with vCard formatted data, it is basically a way to electronically represent widely-used business card data.

Upserting the Information into Force.com with Mobile SDK

Now that you have successfully scanned the tag, you can do a variety of things with the data. In this sample application, you are going to upsert the contact information into the standard Contact object using the Mobile SDK. The method for upserting data is inside the forcetk.js file, which utilizes the Force.com REST API to process data. We use the contact variable we populated in our NFC processing code above as the input into Force.com. Finally, the user initiates the upload into Force.com by clicking the button on the page, although you can easily automate this on the read success method above to make this completely automatic.

```
$j('#insert_lead_from_nfc_tag').click(function(){
    SFHybridApp.logToConsole("Upsert vCard Contact to SFDC " +
        contact.vCard_Email__c + contact.lastName + contact.phone);
    forcetkCli-ent.upsert("Contact","Contact_Ext_ID__c",

contact.contactextid,contact,onSuccessSfdcUpsertContact,onErrorSfdc);

    });
```

After following this use case through completely, if you navigate to the Contacts tab in Force.com and view the recently-added Contacts, you can see the newly-created contact from our NFC tag!

Wrap Up - The Internet of Things and the Future of NFC

As you can see from this simple application, using NFC tags and smartphones opens up a whole world of possibilities for The Internet of Things. For those unfamiliar with the concept, it boils down to real-world objects representing themselves automatically on the Internet. For example, the business card had an NFC tag attached to it, and via your application, automatically communicated its data to our application. This allowed you to easily represent that real-world object in a Salesforce.com org.

You can tag almost anything and track that object in Salesforce. You can tag marketing kiosks to allow users to process leads at a conferencing event. You can set up tags in your business to allow customers to scan products and add them to their shopping lists, or even pay for them automatically via their smartphone, streamlining the whole checkout and purchase process. If you live in the city and take public transit, imagine replacing the transit card in your pocket with an application on your smartphone.

Chapter 11

Distributing Mobile AppExchange Apps

Apps have completely redefined the mobile experience. When selecting a new smartphone or a tablet, consumers consistently rate app availability as the most import factor in their decision. So naturally, after you've developed your mobile app, you'll want to make it available so customers or staff can easily find, buy it, and install it. Android and iOS have proprietary stores that list and distribute mobile apps, which won't be covered in this guide. Salesforce also has a marketplace called the AppExchange, where partners can list mobile apps and consulting services for Salesforce.

AppExchange for Mobile: Enterprise Mobile Apps

With almost half a million mobile app listings in consumer app stores, discovering the perfect enterprise app that is secure, trusted, and works within the Salesforce ecosystem can be a frustrating process. To help our customers find the perfect mobile app and to help developers reach millions of active Salesforce users, go to `http://www.appexchange.com` — the first cross-platform marketplace dedicated to enterprise mobile apps.

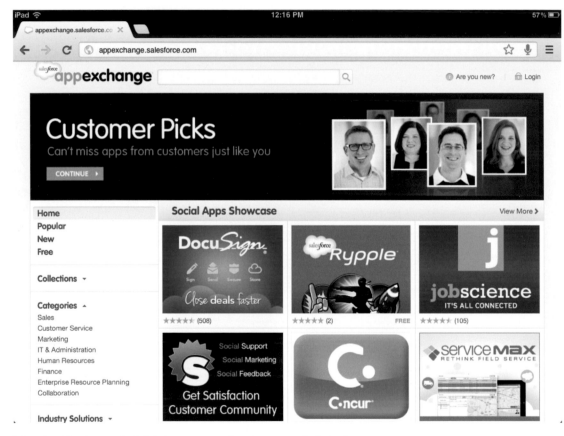

The AppExchange fo Mobile connects developers with Salesforce users.

- Salesforce users can discover brand new mobile apps that are trusted, work with an existing account, and leverage data that's already in the cloud.
- ISVs can list their native, hybrid, and HTML5 applications that work on Android, iOS, and other platforms in a central repository. It doesn't matter whether the app is free, has a fixed price, or is sold with a subscription model.

Whether you're a developer that is working on a special purpose app that brings a unique mobile perspective for solving a specific problem, or a complete solution for a specific role, the space is completely open.

In order to distribute your commercial mobile app on AppExchange, you'll need to become a Salesforce partner.

1. Join the AppExchange Partner Program.
2. Log a case in the Partner Portal for a publishing org.
3. Create your Provider Profile on AppExchange.
4. Request a security review.
5. Log a case in the Partner Portal to request your app is listed on AppExchange for Mobile.

Note: If you're a Salesforce admin creating mobile apps for distribution within your organization, you don't need a public listing on the AppExchange.

Joining the AppExchange Partner Program

The first thing you need to do is join the AppExchange Partner Program. This program is designed to help independent software vendors (ISVs) be successful on the Salesforce platform.

1. In your browser go to www.salesforce.com/partners and click **Join Now**.
2. Select the first option: I want to build and market apps built on the Force.com platform (AppExchange Partner Program)
3. Answer questions about your application and your target market.
4. Fill in the fields about you and your company.
5. In the Additional Questions area, click the drop-down boxes and select the appropriate answer.
6. Enter the Captcha words shown and click **Submit Registration**.
7. In a moment you will receive an email with your username and temporary password. Click the link to the Partner Portal (https://sites.secure.force.com/partners/PP2PartnerLoginPage) and log in.
8. Accept the terms of use and then dismiss the pop-up that appears.
9. Bookmark this page, you'll be using it a lot.

In the Partner Portal you'll see quick links to some of the most used resources, and docs and video to get you started quickly. Most of this information is targeted at ISVs who create add-ons or services for Salesforce users. As a mobile ISV, you'll want to work closely with an AppExchange Partner Program representative.

Get a Publishing Org

In order to manage the distribution and support of your mobile app, you'll want to get a Salesforce organization that has full sales, marketing, and support functionality. This org is called the AppExchange Publishing Org, or APO for short. Qualified partners can get one for free through the Partner Portal.

1. In the Partner Portal, in the Quick Links section, click **Create a Case**.

Figure 1: Create a Case

2. In the Category section, choose the first option.
3. In the first category box, choose **AppExchange and Service Listings**.
4. In the second category box, choose **Request CRM for Partner**.
5. In the Reason drop-down box, choose **Administration Request**.
6. In the Severity drop-down box, choose **High**.
7. In the Subject, enter `Need ISV CRM`.
8. In the Description field, tell us if you have an existing org or if you need a new one. If you have an existing Salesforce org, you can provide the Org ID in the Description field and two additional CRM licenses will be added to your org. If you don't have an existing org, we'll provide a new one for you. In either case, make sure to enter your business address and then click **Save**.

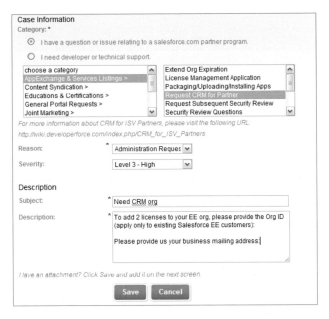

Figure 2: Create a Case in the Partner Portal

9. Shortly, you'll receive another email prompting you to log in and change your password. Do that, and then bookmark the page as before.

Create a Provider Profile

A provider profile represents your company on the AppExchange. You'll need to log into the Salesforce organization where you'll manage your business. If you're a qualified partner, you might already have an APO org. If not, you can use the Developer Edition org.

1. On the login page, use your username and password for your AppExchange Publishing Organziation (APO).
2. Fill out the information in the Provider Profile and then click **Save**.

The AppExchange Security Review

Before you can list an app on AppExchange, you'll need to submit your app for a security review. The fastest way through the security review is to fully understand the security guidelines and process, which is online at http://wiki.developerforce.com/page/Security_Review.

The following procedure is for submitting packaged applications, but the steps are the same for mobile apps. After you submit the form, a representative will contact you for next steps.

1. Click **Start Review** on the Offering tab when editing the listing.
2. Select whether you charge for your application or if your application is free. Free applications must complete the review, but the review fee is waived.
3. If you charge for your application, Partner Operations will email you information within two business days on how to pay for the review. This is an annual payment.
4. Indicate if your application integrates with any web services outside of Force.com, including your own servers.
5. If your application integrates with other web services, list all of them in the `Webservices Used` box. You can enter up to 1000 characters.
6. If your application integrates with other web services, select how your application authenticates with those services. Enter any helpful comments in the box provided. You can enter up to 1000 characters.
7. Indicate if your application stores salesforce.com user credentials outside of Force.com.
8. Indicate if your application stores salesforce.com customer data outside of Force.com.
9. If your application stores salesforce.com customer data outside of Force.com, list all salesforce.com objects accessed in the `Objects Accessed` box. You can enter up to 255 characters.
10. Indicate if your application requires that customers install any client components, such as software or plug-ins.
11. If your application requires client components, enter the details in the `Requirements` box. You can enter up to 1000 characters.
12. Click **Start Security Review** to start the AppExchange Security Review. To discard your changes and return to the previous page, click **Cancel**.

 Note: After collecting payment, the security team will send the partner a survey to collect detailed information on how to test their app. This will include information like install links, test credentials etc. that are mentioned in the next section.

13. You are contractually required to keep this information current. For example, if you upgrade your app to use a new web service, you must edit the information in your

security review submission. To edit your submission information, click **Edit Review** on the Offering tab when editing the listing. Apps are reviewed again periodically.

Mobile apps have additional security steps, and you'll need to provide the following, depending on the phone type:

- iOS Mobile app — Provide the install link if the application is free and already published to the Appstore. If the application is not yet approved or is not free, please either provide an ad-hoc installation (contact us for device UDIDs), or a Testflight link for the app. (no UDID required). More information about Testflight is available at: https://testflightapp.com/. If credentials other than the Salesforce account login, or related external application credentials are required or optional for the mobile application, please provide them as well. If sample data is required for the application to function, please include a logical set of sample data.

- Android app — Provide the .APK for the android application and the target device. If credentials other than the Salesforce account login, or related external application credentials are required or optional for the mobile application, please provide them as well. If sample data is required for the application to function, please include a logical set of sample data.

Chapter 12

Reference

The Mobile SDK reference documentation is hosted on GitHub, which provides a superior viewing and navigating experience.

http://forcedotcom.github.com/SalesforceMobileSDK-iOS

http://forcedotcom.github.com/SalesforceMobileSDK-Android

REST API Resources

The Salesforce Mobile SDK simplifies using the REST API by creating wrappers. All you need to do is call a method and provide the correct parameters; the rest is done for you. This table lists the resources available and what they do. For more information, see the REST API Developer's Guide.

Resource Name	URI	Description
Versions	/	Lists summary information about each Salesforce version currently available, including the version, label, and a link to each version's root.
Resources by Version	/vXX.X/	Lists available resources for the specified API version, including resource name and URI.
Describe Global	/vXX.X/sobjects/	Lists the available objects and their metadata for your organization's data.
SObject Basic Information	/vXX.X/sobjects/**SObject**/	Describes the individual metadata for the specified object. Can also be used to create a new record for a given object.
SObject Describe	/vXX.X/sobjects/**SObject**/describe/	Completely describes the individual metadata at all levels for the specified object.
SObject Rows	/vXX.X/sobjects/**SObject**/**id**/	Accesses records based on the specified object ID. Retrieves, updates, or deletes records. This resource can also be used to retrieve field values.
SObject Rows by External ID	/vXX.X/sobjects/**SObjectName**/ **fieldName**/ **fieldValue**	Creates new records or updates existing records (upserts records) based on the value of a specified external ID field.

Resource Name	URI	Description
SObject Blob Retrieve	/vXX.X/sobjects/**SObject**/**id**/**blobField**	Retrieves the specified blob field from an individual record.
SObject User Password	/vXX.X/sobjects/User/ **user id**/password /vXX.X/sobjects/SelfServiceUser/ **self service user id**/password	Set, reset, or get information about a user password.
Query	/vXX.X/query/?q=**soql**	Executes the specified SOQL query.
Search	/vXX.X/search/?s=**sosl**	Executes the specified SOSL search. The search string must be URL-encoded.

iOS Architecture

At a high level, the current facilities that the native SDK provides to consumers are:

- OAuth authentication capabilities
- REST API communication capabilities
- SmartStore secure storage and retrieval of app data

 Note: This is not currently exposed to native template apps, but is included in the binary distribution.

The Salesforce native SDK is essentially one library, with dependencies on (and providing exposure to) the following additional libraries:

- `libRestKit.a` — Third-party underlying libraries for facilitating REST API calls.
  - ◊ RestKit in turn depends on `libxml2.dylib`, which is part of the standard iOS development environment
- `libSalesforceOAuth.a` — Underlying libraries for managing OAuth authentication.

- `libsqlite3.dylib` — Library providing access to SQLite capabilities. This is also a part of the standard iOS development environment.
- `fmdb` — Objective-C wrapper around SQLite.

 Note: This is not currently exposed to native template apps, but exposed in the binary distribution.

Native iOS Objects

The following objects are important for leveraging Mobile SDK functionality in your app:

- `SFRestAPI`
- `SFRestAPI` (Blocks)
- `SFRestRequest`

SFRestAPI

`SFRestAPI` is the entry point for making REST requests, and is generally accessed as a singleton, via `SFRestAPI sharedInstance`.

You can easily create many standard canned queries from this object, such as:

```
SFRestRequest* request = [[SFRestAPI sharedInstance]
requestForUpdateWithObjectType:@"Contact"
    objectId:contactId
    fields:updatedFields];
```

You can then initiate the request with the following:

```
[[SFRestAPI sharedInstance] send:request delegate:self];
```

SFRestAPI **(Blocks)**

This is a category extension of the `SFRestAPI` class that allows you to specify blocks as your callback mechanism. For example:

```
NSMutableDictionary *fields = [NSMutableDictionary
dictionaryWithObjectsAndKeys:
    @"John", @"FirstName",
    @"Doe", @"LastName",
    nil];
[[SFRestAPI sharedInstance] performCreateWithObjectType:@"Contact"
    fields:fields
    failBlock:^(NSError *e) {
    NSLog(@"Error: %@", e);
    }
```

```
    completeBlock:^(NSDictionary *d) {
        NSLog(@"ID value for object: %@", [d objectForKey:@"id"]);
    }];
```

SFRestRequest

In addition to the canned REST requests provided by SFRestAPI, you can also create your own:

```
NSString *path = @"/v23.0";
SFRestRequest* request = [SFRestRequest
requestWithMethod:SFRestMethodGET path:path queryParams:nil];
```

Other Objects

Though you won't likely leverage these objects directly, their purpose in the SDK is worth noting.

- RKRequestDelegateWrapper—The intermediary between SFRestAPI and the RestKit libraries. RKRequestDelegateWrapper wraps the functionality of RestKit communications, providing convenience methods for determining the type of HTTP post, handling data transformations, and interpreting responses.
- SFSessionRefresher—Tightly-coupled with SFRestAPI, providing an abstraction around functionality for automatically refreshing a session if any REST requests fail due to session expiration.

Android Architecture

The SalesforceSDK is provided as a JAR file of java classes that works in conjunction with a set of libraries and resource files in the native/SalesforceSDK directory.

Java Code

Java sources are under /src.

Package Name	Description
com.salesforce.androidsdk.app	SDK application classes (ForceApp)
com.salesforce.androidsdk.auth	OAuth support classes
com.salesforce.androidsdk.phonegap	Native implementations of the Salesforce Mobile SDK PhoneGap plugin
com.salesforce.androidsdk.rest	Classes for REST requests/responses

Package Name	Description
com.salesforce.androidsdk.security	Security-related helper classes (e.g. passcode manager)
com.salesforce.androidsdk.store	SmartStore and supporting classes
com.salesforce.androidsdk.ui	Activities (e.g. login)
com.salesforce.androidsdk.util	Miscellaneous utility classes

Libraries

Libraries are under /libs.

Library Name	Description
phonegap-1.2.0.jar	Open source mobile development framework; used in hybrid applications (*)
sqlcipher.jar	Open source extension to SQLite that provides transparent 256-bit AES encryptiong of database files (**)
armeabi/*.so	Native libaries required by sqlcipher (**)
commons-code.jar, guava-r09.jar	Java libraries required by sqlcipher

(*) denotes files required for hybrid application.

(**) denotes files required for SmartStore.

Resources

Resources are under /res.

File	Use
edit_icon.png	Server picker screen
glare.png	Login screen
icon.png	Application icon

Folder	File	Use
drawable-hdpi, drawable-ldpi	edit_icon.png	Server picker screen

Folder	File	Use
drawable-hdpi, drawable-ldpi	glare.png	Login screen
drawable-hdpi, drawable-ldpi	icon.png	Application icon
drawable	header_bg.png	Login screen
drawable	progress_spinner.xml	Login screen
drawable	toolbar_background.xml	Login screen
drawable-xlarge, drawable-xlarge-port	header_bg.png	Login screen (tablet)
drawable-xlarge, drawable-xlarge-port	header_drop_shadow.xml	Login screen (tablet)
drawable-xlarge, drawable-xlarge-port	header_left_border.xml	Login screen (tablet)
drawable-xlarge, drawable-xlarge-port	header_refresh.png	Login screen (tablet)
drawable-xlarge, drawable-xlarge-port	header_refresh_press.png	Login screen (tablet)
drawable-xlarge, drawable-xlarge-port	header_refresh_states.xml	Login screen (tablet)
drawable-xlarge, drawable-xlarge-port	header_right_border.xml	Login screen (tablet)
drawable-xlarge, drawable-xlarge-port	login_content_header.xml	Login screen (tablet)
drawable-xlarge, drawable-xlarge-port	nav_shadow.png	Login screen (tablet)
drawable-xlarge, drawable-xlarge-port	oauth_background.png	Login screen (tablet)
drawable-xlarge, drawable-xlarge-port	oauth_container_dropshadow.9.png	Login screen (tablet)
drawable-xlarge, drawable-xlarge-port	oauth_background.png	Login screen (tablet)
drawable-xlarge, drawable-xlarge-port	progress_spinner.xml	Login screen (tablet)

Folder	File	Use
`drawable-xlarge`, `drawable-xlarge-port`	`refresh_loader.png`	Login screen (tablet)
`drawable-xlarge`, `drawable-xlarge-port`	`toolbar_background.xml`	Login screen (tablet)
`layout`	`custom_server_url.xml`	Server picker screen
`layout`	`login.xml`	Login screen
`layout`	`passcode.xml`	Pin screen
`layout`	`server_picker.xml`	Server picker screen
`layout-xlarge`	`login_header.xml`	Login screen (tablet)
`layout-xlarge`	`login.xml`	Login screen (tablet)
`layout-xlarge`	`server_picker_header.xml`	Server picker screen (tablet)
`layout-xlarge`	`server_picker.xml`	Server picker screen (tablet)
`menu`	`clear_custom_url.xml`	Add connection dialog
`menu`	`login.xml`	Login menu (phone)
`values`	`sdk.xml`	Localized strings for login, server picker and pin screens
`values`	`strings.xml`	Other strings (app name)
`values-xlarge`	`styles.xml`	Styles (tablet)
`xml`	`authenticator.xml`	Preferences for account used by application
`xml`	`plugins.xml`	Plugin configuration file for PhoneGap (*)

Java Code

Java sources are under `/src`.

Java Code

Package Name	Description
com.salesforce.androidsdk.app	SDK application classes (ForceApp)
com.salesforce.androidsdk.auth	OAuth support classes
com.salesforce.androidsdk.phonegap	Native implementation of Salesforce Mobile SDK PhoneGap plugin
com.salesforce.androidsdk.rest	Classes for REST requests/responses
com.salesforce.androidsdk.security	Security-related helper classes (e.g. passcode manager)
com.salesforce.androidsdk.store	SmartStore and supporting classes
com.salesforce.androidsdk.ui	Activities (e.g. login)
com.salesforce.androidsdk.util	Miscellaneous utility classes

com.salesforce.androidsdk.app

Class	Description
ForceApp	Abstract subclass of application; you must supply a concrete subclass in your project.

com.salesforce.androidsdk.auth

Class	Description
AuthenticatorService	Service taking care of authentication
HttpAccess	Generic HTTP access layer
OAuth2	Helper class for common OAuth2 requests

com.salesforce.androidsdk.phonegap

Class	Description
SalesforceOAuthPlugin	PhoneGap plugin for Salesforce OAuth
SmartStorePlugin	PhoneGap plugin for SmartStore
TestRunnerPlugin	PhoneGap plugin to run javascript tests in container

com.salesforce.androidsdk.rest

Class	Description
ClientManager	Factory of RestClient, kicks off login flow if needed
RestClient	Authenticated client to talk to a Force.com server
RestRequest	Force.com REST request wrapper
RestResponse	REST response wrapper

com.salesforce.androidsdk.security

Class	Description
Encryptor	Helper class for encryption/decryption/hash computations
PasscodeManager	Inactivity timeout manager, kicks off passcode screen if needed

com.salesforce.androidsdk.store

Class	Description
Database	Encrypted/regular sqlite database wrapper
DBOpenHelper	Helper class to manage regular database creation and version management
DBOperations	DBOpenHelper/EncryptedDBOpenHelper wrapper
EncryptedDBOpenHelper	Helper class to manage encrypted database creation and version management
SmartStore	Searchable/secure store for JSON documents

com.salesforce.androidsdk.ui

Class	Description
CustomServerUrlEditor	Custom dialog allowing user to pick a different login host
LoginActivity	Login screen

Class	Description
OAuthWebviewHelper	Helper class to manage a WebView instance that is going through the OAuth login process
PasscodeActivity	Passcode (PIN) screen
SalesforceDroidGapActivity	Main activity for hybrid applications
SalesforceGapViewClient	WebView client used in hybrid applications
SalesforceR	Class that allows references to resources defined outside the SDK
ServerPickerActivity	Choose login host screen

com.salesforce.androidsdk.util

Class	Description
EventsObservable	Used to register and receive events generated by the SDK (used primarily in tests)
EventsObserver	Observer of SDK events
UriFragmentParser	Helper class for parsing URI's query strings

Libraries

Libraries are under /libs.

Library Name	Description
phonegap-1.2.0.jar	Open source mobile development framework; used in hybrid applications (*)
sqlcipher.jar	Open source extension to SQLite that provides transparent 256-bit AES encryptiong of database files (**)
armeabi/*.so	Native libaries required by sqlcipher (**)
commons-code.jar, guava-r09.jar	Java libarries required by sqlcipher

Resources

Resources are under /res.

drawable-hdpi, drawable-ldpi

File	Use
edit_icon.png	Server picker screen
glare.png	Login screen
icon.png	Application icon

drawable

File	Use
header_bg.png	Login screen
progress_spinner.xml	Login screen
toolbar_background.xml	Login screen

drawable-xlarge, drawable-xlarge-port

File	Use
header_bg.png	Login screen (tablet)
header_drop_shadow.xml	Login screen (tablet)
header_left_border.xml	Login screen (tablet)
header_refresh.png	Login screen (tablet)
header_refresh_press.png	Login screen (tablet)
header_refresh_states.xml	Login screen (tablet)
header_right_border.xml	Login screen (tablet)
login_content_header.xml	Login screen (tablet)
nav_shadow.png	Login screen (tablet)
oauth_background.png	Login screen (tablet)

File	Use
`oauth_container_dropshadow.9.png`	Login screen (tablet)
`oauth_background.png`	Login screen (tablet)
`progress_spinner.xml`	Login screen (tablet)
`refresh_loader.png`	Login screen (tablet)
`toolbar_background.xml`	Login screen (tablet)

`layout`

File	Use
`custom_server_url.xml`	Server picker screen
`login.xml`	Login screen
`passcode.xml`	Pin screen
`server_picker.xml`	Server picker screen

`layout-xlarge`

File	Use
`login_header.xml`	Login screen (tablet)
`login.xml`	Login screen (tablet)
`server_picker_header.xml`	Server picker screen (tablet)
`server_picker.xml`	Server picker screen (tablet)

`menu`

File	Use
`clear_custom_url.xml`	Add connection dialog
`login.xml`	Login menu (phone)

values

File	Use
sdk.xml	Localized strings for login, server picker, and pin screens
strings.xml	Other strings (app name)

values-xlarge

File	Use
styles.xml	Styles (tablet)

xml

File	Use
authenticator.xml	Preferences for account used by application
plugins.xml	Plugin configuration file for PhoneGap. Required for hybrid.

Glossary

A

Access Token

A value used by the consumer to gain access to protected resources on behalf of the user, instead of using the user's Salesforce credentials. The access token is a session ID, and can be used directly.

Account

An *account* is an organization, company, or consumer that you want to track—for example, a customer, partner, or competitor.

Activity, Chatter

An indicator of a person's activity in Chatter. Chatter activity statistics show the number of posts and comments a person has made and the number of comments and likes received.

Administrator (System Administrator)

One or more individuals in your organization who can configure and customize the application. Users assigned to the System Administrator profile have administrator privileges.

Apex

Apex is a strongly typed, object-oriented programming language that allows developers to execute flow and transaction control statements on the Force.com platform server in conjunction with calls to the Force.com API. Using syntax that looks like Java and acts like database stored procedures, Apex enables developers to add business logic to most system events, including button clicks, related record updates, and Visualforce pages. Apex code can be initiated by Web service requests and from triggers on objects.

Apex Controller

See Controller, Visualforce.

App

Short for "application." A collection of components such as tabs, reports, dashboards, and Visualforce pages that address a specific business need. Salesforce provides standard apps such as Sales and Call Center. You can customize the standard apps to match the way you work. In addition, you can package an app and upload it to the AppExchange along with related components such as custom fields, custom tabs, and custom objects. Then, you can make the app available to other Salesforce users from the AppExchange.

AppExchange

The AppExchange is a sharing interface from salesforce.com that allows you to browse and share apps and services for the Force.com platform.

AppExchange Listing

An AppExchange listing is a description of your app or service on the AppExchange. It is your primary marketing tool for promoting your app or service to the AppExchange community.

AppExchange Publishing Organization

The AppExchange Publishing Organization (APO) is the master organization that you as a partner use to publish listings on the AppExchange. Child organizations where you develop applications can be linked to your APO, thus tying your listings together under a single provider entity to deliver a consistent message to customers.

AppExchange Security Review

The AppExchange Security Review ensures that an app is safe for customers to install. Before an app can be listed publicly on theAppExchange it must pass the AppExchange Security Review. Providers are obligated to resubmit an app for security review whenever the app is updated.

AppExchange Upgrades

Upgrading an app is the process of installing a newer version.

Application Programming Interface (API)

The interface that a computer system, library, or application provides to allow other computer programs to request services from it and exchange data.

Authorization Code

A short-lived token that represents the access granted by the end user. The authorization code is used to obtain an access token and a refresh token.

C

Chatter Feed

A list of recent activities in Salesforce. Chatter feeds display:

- On the Chatter or Home tab, where you can see your posts, posts from people you follow, and updates to records you follow, and posts to groups you're a member of
- On profiles, where you can see posts made by the person whose profile you're viewing
- On records, where you can see updates to the record you're viewing
- On Chatter groups, where you can see posts to the group you're viewing

Chatter Mobile

A free mobile application that lets you collaborate in Chatter from your mobile device. Use Chatter Mobile to post and comment in Chatter, and receive updates about the people, records, and files you follow and your groups.

Child Relationship

A relationship that has been defined on an sObject that references another sObject as the "one" side of a one-to-many relationship. For example, contacts, opportunities, and tasks have child relationships with accounts.

See also sObject.

Class, Apex

A template or blueprint from which Apex objects are created. Classes consist of other classes, user-defined methods, variables, exception types, and static initialization code. In most cases, Apex classes are modeled on their counterparts in Java.

Client App

An app that runs outside the Salesforce user interface and uses only the Force.com API or Bulk API. It typically runs on a desktop or mobile device. These apps treat the platform as a data source, using the development model of whatever tool and platform for which they are designed.

Cloud Computing

A model for software development and distribution based on the Internet. The technology infrastructure for a service, including data, is hosted on the Internet. This allows consumers to develop and use services with browsers or other thin clients instead of investing in hardware, software, or maintenance.

Component, Visualforce

Something that can be added to a Visualforce page with a set of tags, for example, `<apex:detail>`. Visualforce includes a number of standard components, or you can create your own custom components.

Component Reference, Visualforce

A description of the standard and custom Visualforce components that are available in your organization. You can access the component library from the development footer of any Visualforce page or the *Visualforce Developer's Guide*.

Consumer Key

A value used by the consumer to identify itself to Salesforce. Referred to as `client_id`.

Controller, Visualforce

An Apex class that provides a Visualforce page with the data and business logic it needs to run. Visualforce pages can use the standard controllers that come by default with every standard or custom object, or they can use custom controllers.

Custom Field

A field that can be added in addition to the standard fields to customize Salesforce for your organization's needs.

Custom Object

Custom records that allow you to store information unique to your organization.

D

Database

An organized collection of information. The underlying architecture of the Force.com platform includes a database where your data is stored.

Dependent Field

Any custom picklist or multi-select picklist field that displays available values based on the value selected in its corresponding controlling field.

Developer Edition

A free, fully-functional Salesforce organization designed for developers to extend, integrate, and develop with the Force.com platform. Developer Edition accounts are available on developer.force.com.

Developer Force

The Developer Force website at developer.force.com provides a full range of resources for platform developers, including sample code, toolkits, an online developer community, and the ability to obtain limited Force.com platform environments.

Development Environment

A Salesforce organization where you can make configuration changes that will not affect users on the production organization. There are two kinds of development environments, sandboxes and Developer Edition organizations.

Dynamic Visualforce Binding

A way of writing generic Visualforce pages that display information about records without necessarily knowing which fields to show. In other words, fields on the page are determined at runtime, rather than compile time.

E

Enterprise Edition

A Salesforce edition designed for larger, more complex businesses.

Enterprise WSDL

A strongly-typed WSDL for customers who want to build an integration with their Salesforce organization only, or for partners who are using tools like Tibco or webMethods to build integrations that require strong typecasting. The downside of the Enterprise WSDL is that it only works with the schema of a single Salesforce organization because it is bound to all of the unique objects and fields that exist in that organization's data model.

F

Feed Attachment, Chatter

A feed attachment is a file or link that is attached to a post in a Chatter feed.

Feed Filter, Chatter

Feed filters display a subset of posts in your Chatter feed on the Chatter tab.

Feed Tracking, Chatter

Administrator settings that determine which records can be followed and which fields can be tracked in Chatter feeds. Enabling an object for feed tracking allows people to follow records of that object type. Enabling fields for feed tracking allows users to see updates on the Chatter feed when those fields are changed on records they follow.

Field

A part of an object that holds a specific piece of information, such as a text or currency value.

Field Dependency

A filter that allows you to change the contents of a picklist based on the value of another field.

Field-Level Security

Settings that determine whether fields are hidden, visible, read only, or editable for users. Available in Enterprise, Unlimited, and Developer Editions only.

Field Sets

A field set is a grouping of fields. For example, you could have a field set that contains fields describing a user's first name, middle name, last name, and business title. Field sets can be referenced on Visualforce pages dynamically. If the page is added to a managed package, administrators can add, remove, or reorder fields in a field set to modify the fields presented on the Visualforce page without modifying any code.

Force.com

The salesforce.com platform for building applications in the cloud. Force.com combines a powerful user interface, operating system, and database to allow you to customize and deploy applications in the cloud for your entire enterprise.

Force.com App Menu

A menu that enables users to switch between customizable applications (or "apps") with a single click. The Force.com app menu displays at the top of every page in the user interface.

Force.com IDE

An Eclipse plug-in that allows developers to manage, author, debug and deploy Force.com applications in the Eclipse development environment.

Web Services API

A Web services application programming interface that provides access to your Salesforce organization's information. See also SOAP API and Bulk API.

G

Group

A groups is a set of users. Groups can contain individual users, other groups, or the users in a role. Groups can be used to help define sharing access to data or to specify which data to synchronize when using Connect for Outlook or Connect for Lotus Notes.

Users can define their own personal groups. Administrators can create public groups for use by everyone in the organization.

Group Edition

A product designed for small businesses and workgroups with a limited number of users.

I

Import Wizard

A tool for importing data into your Salesforce organization, accessible from Setup.

Instance

The cluster of software and hardware represented as a single logical server that hosts an organization's data and runs their applications. The Force.com platform runs on multiple instances, but data for any single organization is always consolidated on a single instance.

Integration User

A Salesforce user defined solely for client apps or integrations. Also referred to as the logged-in user in a SOAP API context.

M

Managed Package

A collection of application components that is posted as a unit on the AppExchange and associated with a namespace and possibly a License Management Organization. To support upgrades, a package must be managed. An organization can create a single managed package that can be downloaded and installed by many different organizations. Managed packages differ from unmanaged packages by having some locked components, allowing the managed package to be upgraded later. Unmanaged packages do not include locked components and cannot be upgraded. In addition, managed packages obfuscate certain components (like Apex) on subscribing organizations to protect the intellectual property of the developer.

Metadata

Information about the structure, appearance, and functionality of an organization and any of its parts. Force.com uses XML to describe metadata.

Metadata-Driven Development

An app development model that allows apps to be defined as declarative "blueprints," with no code required. Apps built on the platform—their data models, objects, forms, workflows, and more—are defined by metadata.

Metadata WSDL

A WSDL for users who want to use the Force.com Metadata API calls.

MVC (Model-View-Controller)

A design paradigm that deconstructs applications into components that represent data (the model), ways of displaying that data in a user interface (the view), and ways of manipulating that data with business logic (the controller).

N

Namespace

In a packaging context, a one- to 15-character alphanumeric identifier that distinguishes your package and its contents from packages of other developers onAppExchange, similar to a domain name. Salesforce automatically prepends your namespace prefix, followed by two underscores ("__"), to all unique component names in your Salesforce organization.

O

Object

An object allows you to store information in your Salesforce organization. The object is the overall definition of the type of information you are storing. For example, the case object allow you to store information regarding customer inquiries. For each object, your organization will have multiple records that store the information about specific instances of that type of data. For example, you might have a case record to store the information about Joe Smith's training inquiry and another case record to store the information about Mary Johnson's configuration issue.

Organization

A deployment of Salesforce with a defined set of licensed users. An organization is the virtual space provided to an individual customer of salesforce.com. Your organization includes all of your data and applications, and is separate from all other organizations.

Organization-Wide Defaults

Settings that allow you to specify the baseline level of data access that a user has in your organization. For example, you can set organization-wide defaults so that any user can see any record of a particular object that is enabled via their object permissions, but they need extra permissions to edit one.

P

Package

A group of Force.com components and applications that are made available to other organizations through the AppExchange. You use packages to bundle an app along with any related components so that you can upload them to AppExchange together.

Permission

A permission is a setting that allows a user to perform certain functions in Salesforce. Permissions can be enabled in permission sets and profiles. Examples of permissions include the "Edit" permission on a custom object and the "Modify All Data" permission.

Permission Set

A collection of permissions and settings that gives users access to specific tools and functions.

Production Organization

A Salesforce organization that has live users accessing data.

Profile

Defines a user's permission to perform different functions within Salesforce. For example, the Solution Manager profile gives a user access to create, edit, and delete solutions.

R

Record

A single instance of a Salesforce object. For example, "John Jones" might be the name of a contact record.

Record-Level Security

A method of controlling data in which you can allow a particular user to view and edit an object, but then restrict the records that the user is allowed to see.

Refresh Token

A token used by the consumer to obtain a new access token, without having the end user approve the access again.

Remote Access Application

A *remote access application* is an application external to Salesforce that uses the OAuth protocol to verify both the Salesforce user and the external application.

REST API

REST is a simple, lightweight API that uses HTTP GET, POST and PUT methods to update resources on the server.

S

IdeaExchange

A forum where salesforce.com customers can suggest new product concepts, promote favorite enhancements, interact with product managers and other customers, and preview what salesforce.com is planning to deliver in future releases. Visit IdeaExchange at ideas.salesforce.com.

Salesforce SOA (Service-Oriented Architecture)

A powerful capability of Force.com that allows you to make calls to external Web services from within Apex.

Sandbox Organization

> A nearly identical copy of a Salesforce production organization. You can create multiple sandboxes in separate environments for a variety of purposes, such as testing and training, without compromising the data and applications in your production environment.

Session ID

> An authentication token that is returned when a user successfully logs in to Salesforce. The Session ID prevents a user from having to log in again every time he or she wants to perform another action in Salesforce. Different from a record ID or Salesforce ID, which are terms for the unique ID of a Salesforce record.

Session Timeout

> The period of time after login before a user is automatically logged out. Sessions expire automatically after a predetermined length of inactivity, which can be configured in Salesforce by clicking **Your Name** > **Setup** > **Security Controls**. The default is 120 minutes (two hours). The inactivity timer is reset to zero if a user takes an action in the Web interface or makes an API call.

Setup

> An administration area where you can customize and define Force.com applications. Access Setup through the **Your Name** > **Setup** link at the top of Salesforce pages.

Sharing

> Allowing other users to view or edit information you own. There are different ways to share data:
>
> - Sharing Model—defines the default organization-wide access levels that users have to each other's information and whether to use the hierarchies when determining access to data.
> - Role Hierarchy—defines different levels of users such that users at higher levels can view and edit information owned by or shared with users beneath them in the role hierarchy, regardless of the organization-wide sharing model settings.
> - Sharing Rules—allow an administrator to specify that all information created by users within a given group or role is automatically shared to the members of another group or role.
> - Manual Sharing—allows individual users to share records with other users or groups.

- Apex-Managed Sharing—enables developers to programmatically manipulate sharing to support their application's behavior. See Apex-Managed Sharing.

Sharing Model

Behavior defined by your administrator that determines default access by users to different types of records.

SOAP (Simple Object Access Protocol)

A protocol that defines a uniform way of passing XML-encoded data.

SOQL (Salesforce Object Query Language)

A query language that allows you to construct simple but powerful query strings and to specify the criteria that should be used to select data from the Force.com database.

SOSL (Salesforce Object Search Language)

A query language that allows you to perform text-based searches using the Force.com API.

Standard Object

A built-in object included with the Force.com platform. You can also build custom objects to store information that is unique to your app.

System Log

Part of the Developer Console, a separate window console that can be used for debugging code snippets. Enter the code you want to test at the bottom of the window and click Execute. The body of the System Log displays system resource information, such as how long a line took to execute or how many database calls were made. If the code did not run to completion, the console also displays debugging information.

T

Test Method

An Apex class method that verifies whether a particular piece of code is working properly. Test methods take no arguments, commit no data to the database, and can be executed by the `runTests()` system method either through the command line or in an Apex IDE, such as the Force.com IDE.

Translation Workbench

The Translation Workbench lets you specify languages you want to translate, assign translators to languages, create translations for customizations you've made to your Salesforce organization, and override labels and translations from managed packages. Everything from custom picklist values to custom fields can be translated so your global users can use all of Salesforce in their language.

Trigger

A piece of Apex that executes before or after records of a particular type are inserted, updated, or deleted from the database. Every trigger runs with a set of context variables that provide access to the records that caused the trigger to fire, and all triggers run in bulk mode—that is, they process several records at once, rather than just one record at a time.

U

Unit Test

A unit is the smallest testable part of an application, usually a method. A unit test operates on that piece of code to make sure it works correctly. See also Test Method.

Unlimited Edition

Unlimited Edition is salesforce.com's flagship solution for maximizing CRM success and extending that success across the entire enterprise through the Force.com platform.

Unmanaged Package

A package that cannot be upgraded or controlled by its developer.

URL (Uniform Resource Locator)

The global address of a website, document, or other resource on the Internet. For example, http://www.salesforce.com.

V

Visualforce

A simple, tag-based markup language that allows developers to easily define custom pages and components for apps built on the platform. Each tag corresponds to a coarse or fine-grained component, such as a section of a page, a related list, or a field. The components can either be controlled by the same logic that is used in standard Salesforce pages, or developers can associate their own logic with a controller written in Apex.

W

Web Service

A mechanism by which two applications can easily exchange data over the Internet, even if they run on different platforms, are written in different languages, or are geographically remote from each other.

WebService Method

An Apex class method or variable that can be used by external systems, like a mash-up with a third-party application. Web service methods must be defined in a global class.

WSDL (Web Services Description Language) File

An XML file that describes the format of messages you send and receive from a Web service. Your development environment's SOAP client uses the Salesforce Enterprise WSDL or Partner WSDL to communicate with Salesforce using the SOAP API.

X

XML (Extensible Markup Language)

A markup language that enables the sharing and transportation of structured data. All Force.com components that are retrieved or deployed through the Metadata API are represented by XML definitions.

Index

Index

Index

Notes